divorce

a canadian woman's guide

gail vaz-oxlade

Prentice
Hall
Canada

A Pearson Company

Toronto

Canadian Cataloguing in Publication Data

Vaz-Oxlade, Gail E., 1959-
        Divorce: a Canadian woman's guide

ISBN 0-13-026534-9

1. Divorce – Canada. 2. Divorced women – Canada. I. Title.

HQ838.V39 2000   306'.082'0971   C00-931469-5

ISBN 0-13-026534-9

Editorial Director, Trade Division: Andrea Crozier
Acquisitions Editor: Nicole de Montbrun
Copy Editor: Kat Mototsune
Production Editor: Jodi Lewchuk
Art Direction: Mary Opper
Cover and Interior Design: Julia Hall
Production Manager: Kathrine Pummell
Page Layout: Dave McKay

1 2 3 4 5 W 04 03 02 01 00

Printed and bound in Canada.

This publication contains the opinions and ideas of its author and is designed to provide useful advice in regard to the subject matter covered. The author and publisher are not engaged in rendering legal, accounting, or other professional services in this publication. This publication is not intended to provide a basis for action in particular circumstances without consideration by a competent professional. The author and publisher expressly disclaim any responsibility for any liability, loss, or risk, personal or otherwise, which is incurred as a consequence, directly or indirectly, of the use and application of any of the contents of this book.

Visit the Prentice Hall Canada Web site! Send us your comments, browse our catalogues, and more. **www.phcanada.com**.

Prentice
Hall
Canada

A Pearson Company

To my girls, Amanda and Alexandra.
I hope neither of you ever have need of this book.
I love you both.
Happy hunting.

Contents

Epilogue:

Endnotes   161

Appendices

Thank You

A lot of women helped to make this book happen.

First, there were all you women who generously shared your stories with me. Sometimes it was very painful for you, I know. Sometimes we both cried. Sometimes we laughed. Sometimes you made me aware of things I'd just never thought of, especially when it came to the children. I truly appreciate you opening your hearts and sharing your stories. These stories will help other women see the lessons they need to learn to successfully come through, and bring their children through, divorce. Thank you, thank you.

To my good friend Terry, who read my manuscript. Thanks for the Chinese food and for sharing your girls with me. They are models of how children can come through divorce intact and happy.

To my editor, Nicole de Montbrun, who patiently listened as I worked through some of the kinks I encountered while writing this book. Your support throughout was greatly appreciated.

And, finally, to my husband, Ken. You are the living proof that great husbands do exist. Having tried, tried, and tried again at marriage, I am thrilled to have finally gotten it right. Thank you for allowing me to be me, warts and all. And thank you for listening to the drafts, for all the 4:00 a.m. discussions, and for being my friend.

Special note: To protect the privacy of the women who shared their stories with me, names have been changed, as well as the gender and, in some cases, the number of children.

Introduction

This book stirred in me about three years ago when I was working on my last book, *A Woman of Independent Means*. At the time I was astounded at how little existed in the way of financial advice for women who were coping with divorce. As I waded through tonnes of legalese and financial jargon, it became clear that Canadian women are desperately in need of clear, simple, and sound advice in coping with this devastating life event.

Having finished *A Woman*, my thoughts turned back to the need for a divorce book. So I went shopping to see what was available. A single computer search returned hundreds of titles. Most were not Canadian and, if you haven't heard me say this before, listen up: Canadians can't count on American financial or legal guides. We do not live in the same country. We have different laws, different tax rules, different approaches to life. The few titles I found that were Canadian, while wonderful as reference guides, lacked a certain ease of reading, a certain clarity, and perhaps a recognition that divorce entails an enormous amount of emotion. Because a topic such as divorce has so many legal and financial implications, the tendency is to pack a book full of every eventuality so that all the bases are covered. Yet no author would ever suggest that a book is any kind of substitute for direct advice from a family law specialist

As many people as are going through a divorce, there are as many different ways divorce can be done. Each player brings a unique set of goals, neuroses, and complications to the divorce. And every divorce must be played out according to its own script. That's clear when you read the tales of other women who have already been where you are about to go.

For some, the divorce decision was pushed upon them. For others, the decision was a moment of triumph. For most, living through the ending of one life and the beginning of another took incredible bravery. For no one was it simple. It meant disconnecting her life from another and facing the future alone. It necessitated coping with all the detritus of those married years. It required picking up, dusting off, and starting all over again.

The underlying thread through all the stories is that you are the only person who can set the game plan that will get you to the other end in one piece. There's no question that your journey will be a hard one. Whether you've initiated the divorce, or it has been thrust upon you, you'll likely experience (or have experienced) a period of significant unhappiness as you've struggled with the idea of separation. You will watch as your children suffer through their parents' conflict. But you will come through, as will your children. You will adapt. And you'll develop new routines, perhaps more quickly than you can believe right now. And if you feel you have failed because your marriage is ending, at least you can count among your blessings that you will not have spent your whole life failing.

If you focus solely on the loss created by your divorce, you'll be living in the past. To look to the future you must be willing to hope, to be optimistic of the new possibilities that are opening up.

So here's what I've come up with. It's a book of stories. Stories from women who have come through their divorces in one piece—some just barely. Stories that cover many of the issues you may have to deal with as you work through the reinvention of your own life. Stories that will show you that you are not alone in your worry, your sorrow or your desperation. And woven among the stories are the legal and financial watch-points— traps, quagmires, swamps. The treacherous black ice that is the court system. The muck and sludge through which you may have to tramp as you deal with custody issues. The imbroglio of the financial settlement.

I hope you find this book useful and pertinent to your own unique and very personal journey.

So, You're
Getting a Divorce

Divorce: disunion, disjunction, disconnection, dissolution, separation, severance, breach, split, detachment, disruption, partition.

It is all these things at once. The ending of a union once made in love. The disjunction of a life's path. The disconnection of people, memories, lives. The dissolution of vows. The separation from children, family, and friends. The severance of a partnership. The breach of trust. The split of futures. The detachment that is indifference. The disruption of lives. The partition of...well, everything.

There are books about how bad divorce is, and books about how to make your divorce a good one. There are magazines, web sites, chat groups, television shows, movies, songs—just about every cultural reflector has a take on divorce. Yet divorce is a relatively new phenomenon, which is probably why we still aren't very good at it.

The Western world saw sharp increases in divorce during the twentieth century, as the earlier social, economic, and legal barriers to divorce were stripped away. Divorce rates rose sharply after the Second World War, continued to rise more slowly for a couple of decades, and then climbed steadily through the last third of the century. So, it became not only more normal for people in middle and lower levels of society to consider divorce, it became more affordable.

According to Barbara Dafoe Whitehead in her book *The Divorce Culture*, the late 1950s brought a significant shift in our attitudes, "away from an ethic of obligation to others and toward an obligation to self."[1] That isn't to say that people suddenly abandoned everyone around them, but that they became far more aware of their own needs and what they would have to do to attend to themselves.

In 1951, there was only one divorce for every 24 couples that married—not exactly an epidemic. By 1990, the ratio of divorces to marriages had increased to one divorce per 2.4 marriages; that's a ten-fold increase[2]. The numbers continued to climb until 1994—the last year in which Canadians saw an increase in divorce numbers—when 78,880 Canadian couples divorced, 654 more than in 1993. However, since the increase between 1993 and 1994 was almost insignificant, it did not change the rate of divorce, which remained at 2.7 per 1,000 population. In 1995, the number of divorces declined 1.6 percent to 77,636.

The average age for men divorcing was 40, while for women it was 37. And the average length of a marriage was 12.4 years, belying the "seven year itch" theory. However, traditional marriages aren't the only relationships that end. It is also estimated that roughly 70 percent of first common-law unions ended in separation. Yet, in spite of the high levels of instability in these arrangements, 50 percent of Canadian women born between 1971 and 1980 would likely enter a common-law relationship at some point.[3] So while many people may claim an aversion to marriage because of the high likelihood of divorce, they don't apply the same rationale to entering common-law relationships.

For decades, families that were divorced were characterized as broken, as if divorce in some way made all the members of what was previously a perfectly adjusted "whole" family deviants or screwed up. The stereotyping doesn't stop with the adult participants—unhappy single mothers and gallivanting, irresponsible fathers—innocent children, too, are stigmatized by divorce stereotypes.

I know a young lad of six or so who was the unhappy child of divorce. He acted up. He was mean, rude, and disobedient. He's a beautiful little boy, with large expressive eyes that have an impish twinkle. Everyone around him says his behaviour is a result of the divorce. They sigh and look knowingly at each other. It's to be expected, after all. And it has been his unspoken excuse for all the rotten things he has said and done. I've been dealing with this devil-angel child for two-and-a-half years and I don't make excuses for his bad behaviour. I don't see why he needs to be labelled with the failure of his parents' marriage. So I hold *him* accountable…and surprise! He's stopped directing his frustration—or is it his wrath?—at me.

While society's view of divorce has finally begun to change, much of the old language remains. Naturally, this negative view does nothing to help a family get through the crisis of divorce. On the contrary, as Constance Ahrons, puts it, "It is dangerous to the soul."[4] Ahrons suggests that the language of divorce needs to change so that instead of "broken" families we become "binuclear" families. And instead of dealing with all the "exes" and "steps" that arise through divorce and remarriage, we focus on the positives of the near relatives by calling them "fuzzy kin."

People pitch into the rapids of divorce through one of three streams. He leaves her. She leaves him. Or they leave each other. The swirls and eddies of the trip are remarkably different depending on your starting point. And your ability to cope, your stamina, and your perspective are a reflection of your ability to see into your own future.

Perhaps the most frightening part of the divorce process is the mystery that still surrounds it. Despite the fact that divorce has been termed as rampant, few but the specialists have a clear understanding of the rules, the games and the power-plays that can make the difference between "the good divorce" and "the divorce from hell."

I was twice divorced by the age of 31. My first marriage ended after a year of abuse. My husband was an angry man whom I thought I could rescue. It took a three-year separation for the final dissolution. My second marriage ended when I suddenly woke up—it felt like the light just came on one day—and realized that I was no longer me. I had compromised so much that I was a mere shadow of myself. And I was unhappy. I probably would have left sooner, but I buried myself in all forms of distractions for the last year or so. When the light did come on, I was gone—lickety-split. It took a year for the divorce to become final.

Both divorces were simple. I had no children. In the first case we had no assets, and in the second we didn't fight very hard about the separation of our assets. But those divorces were also hard. After I left my first husband in Australia, I would see him in all manner of other men's faces. I would shiver. It took a good many years to shake the memory of him slamming me up against the wall. When I left my second husband, I missed him so much. I was at once glad to be able to breathe again, and sad for the loss of my future with him.

Ever the optimist, I've married again. I have children now, and a husband I adore. And I realize that from here to there is never a straight line. The meanderings of life's path leave us open to new discoveries—some good, some not so good. I now understand that "Tomorrow is another day" is more than just a sentiment. It is an anthem for a divorcing person, a mantra to be whispered, screamed, howled, ground out between clenched teeth.

Before We Go Further

Trying to give advice to people who are going through divorce is one of the hardest things I've ever had to do. I spent more time noodling on this book—How should I position this? What should I say about that? What do I really believe?—than just about anything else I've written. My husband has spent many an early morning listening to me babble about one or another divorce issue as I tried to figure out the best approach. You see, with different agenda, different styles, different circumstances, almost everyone has a different set of issues to deal with. And no matter what your girlfriend tells you about what she did when she was divorcing, it'll likely have little application to your life.

One of the biggest areas of conflict is between the desire to protect oneself financially and the need to behave like a reasonable, even if devastated, human being; there's the rub. For while I want to tell you to do *whatever* it takes to make sure you and your children have the essentials, I also want to impress upon you how important it is that you be fair, that you not totally eliminate the goodwill you may have left in your relationship with your ex. Under normal circumstances, emptying the joint account is the wrong thing to do. You and your spouse are both entitled to that money, so the most you have the right to take is half. But under circumstances where you have no sources of income and you truly—look deep into your heart girlfriend—feel you and your children are at risk, then I say empty the damn bank account and deal with the fallout later.

What I don't want to do, as I'm writing this book, is have to put a proviso in at every turn. You know, the "if this, then that, but if that, then this" statements that leave everyone wondering what the hell is going on. What I'll have to do, therefore, is put some trust in you, my reader, to accept my advice in the way that it is intended.

So, what is my intent? It is to provide you with information and options to think about as you progress through this difficult time. I do not want to inflame you, but I do want to strongly motivate you to act if you are para-lyzed. I do not want to incite you, but I do want to impress upon you the importance of taking control of the situation. I do not want to hurt you, but I do want to tell you that you cannot be selfish and self-centred if you have children.

I believe that it is any divorcing parents' responsibility to ensure that they do everything in their power to make their children's lives as normal as possible. Now normal may not be "same as it was." With a divorce pend-ing, the old will never again be. But you can achieve a state of balance where both people accept their responsibilities as parents and act in a mature way for the sake of their children.

As my husband and I sat talking early one morning, I was expounding on the way I felt about marriage contracts. I don't like them—emotionally, that is. There's just something about being asked to sign one that rattles my chain. Yet, I believe in my heart that the best time to lay down the rules for a divorce is when you're still happily married—when you can identify your joint beliefs, concerns, and priorities without the stench of a charred heart stinging your nostrils. For it is only when we are seeing eye to eye, when we're in love, that we act selflessly.

When you are divorcing you need to be both selfish and selfless. While you need to protect yourself and your family—you must do whatever it takes to keep your babies safe—you also need to stop from time to time and stand in your partner's boots. How's he feeling about not seeing the kids at bedtime? What's it like for him to be responsible for all the financial stuff while you're getting back on your feet? How would you feel dropping the kids "home" after you'd had a "visit"?

At this point, I don't care if he left you or you left him. No marriage ends because one person is wholly to blame. If you are smug in your self-righteousness, ask yourself this: if you're so wonderful why would he want to leave? Fact is, in any divorce, both parties bear a portion of the responsibility for the marriage's end.

Having said all that, I want you to know that there's nothing more important than being prepared. That means knowing what to expect and knowing what to do to make things come out best. And, that, ultimately, is what this book is about.

Divorce: A Stage-by-Stage Guide

The process of getting a divorce has changed, and will continue to change, as we try to streamline the system, make it more child-focussed, make it less expensive. New processes are introduced, tested, and incorporated or tossed out. Sometimes the new systems introduced make no sense whatsoever—the person who thought it up never actually had to stand in the line to get the court date—so everyone is in pain until someone has the guts to admit the old way worked better. Yet we muddle through. And as we do, we come to realize that the ending of a marriage is far more of a legal event than the beginning. Those words that were spoken in love to a single representative of the law (and of God, perhaps) must be undone by a virtual army.

Depending on where you live in Canada, the process of getting a divorce can be quite different. Here, I've highlighted the main streets. It'll be up to your lawyer to explain the lanes, side streets, and back-alleys of your divorce. If you're lucky, smart, willing, and able, you'll be able to negotiate your way through the maze without becoming too lost in the jungle of motions, continuances and discoveries. If you're unfortunate enough to have to take full advantage of all the law and our court systems have to offer by way of side-streets and detours, you are going to find it very difficult to focus on getting to the end. But that's what you must do. I won't lie to you and tell you that it'll be easy. It won't. But a good lawyer will get you through. And the love of your children can keep you balanced, if you focus on them and on creating a new life together.

Before the Petition for Divorce

Prior to asking or *petitioning* for divorce, couples often resolve many of the legal issues related to the dissolution of their marriage with separation agreements or interim court orders, which are later incorporated into the final divorce order. Without either children or assets, you and your ex may simply go your own way with no formal action being taken unless one of you wishes to remarry.

Even amicable separations should be formalized with a written separation agreement at some point, particularly when children are involved or where there are significant assets or debts. I remember being called by a reporter to comment on the unfairness of a situation where an ex-wife was being held accountable for her ex-husband's debts years after the divorce. The woman had never had her name removed from the loan agreement when her husband assumed the debt so, when he declared bankruptcy, the bank saw her as their only recourse for recapturing their loss. This is a typical example of how we perceive the divorce itself as the finalization of all connections with the past. That's only true if we've put all the pieces in place for the divorce to be finalized. If you haven't done the work to insulate yourself from your prior partner's indiscretions, consider yourself warned: you'll still be on the hook.

At this point, one or both of you may consult a lawyer, a family court counsellor, a court conciliator, or a mediator. Sometimes people decide to try again at their marriage. Did you know that a section of Divorce Act requires legal advisors to discuss the possibility of reconciliation with their clients and to advise them about reconciliation support services? Of course, if you're adamant about a divorce, your reconciliation speech will probably take all of three-and-a-half minutes.

As you negotiate, and before you sign your separation agreement, you should obtain independent legal advice. That means no matter how great the two of you get along, no matter how simple the divorce, no matter how far he's bending over to accommodate you, you can't use the same lawyer.

Agreements are often negotiated between the two lawyers. You tell your lawyer who tells the other lawyer who tells your ex, who tells his lawyer who tells your lawyer who then tells you. No wonder divorce takes so long and is so damn expensive! If you can't come to an agreement, your lawyers may refer you to a mediator skilled in helping angry people come to a resolution.

Once you've signed the agreement, you can begin divorce proceedings immediately. Or you can do nothing further until one or the other of you wishes to divorce, perhaps to remarry.

If, after the involvement of counsellors, mediators, your lawyers, and whomever else you have stirred into your divorce mix, the both of you still cannot agree, applications can be made to the court to resolve the issues. Each province and territory has legislation permitting the courts to deal with issues of custody, child support, spousal support, possession of the matrimonial home, and division of property.

The actual Divorce Petition requires a lot of information. You can help your lawyer and save time if you already have it all available. See the Divorce Petition Checklist (Appendix B) for the information you should start gathering. You will also need to file a certified copy of your marriage certificate and a certified copy of the Decree Absolute or Divorce Judgment if either of you have gone the divorce route before.

The Divorce Proceeding

When you and/or your ex file an application with the court, the process of divorcing begins. This Petition for Divorce usually describes the length of the marriage, the legal grounds for seeking the divorce, the income and assets of the applicant spouse, and the children of the marriage. Custody, as well as child and spousal support are also proposed. Applications for the division of property (governed by provincial or territorial statutes) are often joined with the divorce petition. Some provincial or territorial rules require an application for property division to be made in separate documents, but permit it to be heard at the same time as the divorce petition. Other jurisdictions' rules permit property claims to be included directly in the divorce petition. Occasionally, an application for property division has already been made and decided before the divorce proceedings begin.

The *petitioner* is the person asking for the divorce; the *respondent* is the spouse who is being divorced. While you can file a petition before you've been separated for a year, your divorce won't be granted until that one-year period has elapsed if separation has been given as your grounds for divorce. Once filed in court, the petition is then served on the respondent who has a specified time in which to answer the petition. If you don't know where to serve your ex, there is a provision that allows for the notification through advertisements placed in newspapers. This is how I divorced my first ex when he was living in Australia since, after I flew the coop, I had no idea where he was.

A response isn't usually filed if the petition includes the terms of a signed separation agreement. Nor is a response given when the respondent agrees with the petition. Only in cases where the divorce is being contested does a response come into play. According to a report by the Canadian Department of Justice, less than 4 percent of divorces are finalized by a contested hearing in Canada.[5] In most jurisdictions, an uncontested petition can proceed without an oral hearing. A judge reviews the documents and makes a divorce judgment.

If neither party appeals the divorce judgment, it takes effect in 31 days. If there is an order regarding matters such as child support, custody, and access as part of the judgment, this part of the judgment may take effect immediately.

If the respondent contests the divorce, the petitioner will be given an opportunity to respond. Now we're into big time negotiations, mediation, whatever it takes to resolve the disputes. In some provinces, a pre-trial hearing is required to mediate a settlement or, at the very least, obtain agreement on as many issues as possible in order to reduce the length of the trial. If the disputed issues are resolved, the divorce will proceed as if it were uncontested. If issues are not resolved, an answer is filed and the divorce is then contested.

Whenever important issues, such as custody, child and spousal support, or possession of the matrimonial home, cannot be resolved quickly your lawyer will suggest you file for interim orders. Examinations for discovery, during which each spouse is questioned by the other's lawyer, are held so each side can question the other party under oath in preparation for trial. Disputes regarding custody or access to the children will usually result in an assessment by a psychiatrist, psychologist, or social worker.

Everyone keeps negotiating all through this process. If at any time everyone can come to an agreement, you can draw up and sign a separation agreement and get divorced. If, after discoveries, you and your ex still can't see eye to eye, a trial will be ordered. During this trial, each party presents evidence on each of the issues in dispute. The judge then makes the final decision. The judge's rulings on child support and other issues are included in the divorce order and, if no appeal is filed, you'll be divorced 31 days later.

The Divorce Act makes a distinction between the act of freeing you from the legal ties of marriage and finalizing a variety of other issues, including spousal support, child support, custody and access, and equalization; therefore, you can actually get a divorce and remarry before all the other "collateral issues" are resolved.

Francine's Story

Aaron and I divorced more than six years ago. Since then, I've had total responsibility for the kids. He doesn't even see them. It's been a huge fight to get him to pay his child support. And since he moved to New York, it's been a nightmare. Two years ago he married again and he now has two other children. My kids don't have a dad and I haven't been able to get my financial house in order. I can't even sell this house and move on because we have yet to equalize. He has been such a bastard. It's been fine for him. He has plenty of money and has a new life. I am stranded in my past with no idea how I'm every going to get on with my life. I feel absolutely lost. The court system has been a joke. The system has failed me, my lawyer has screwed up royally and my life is progressing, without me.

Discoveries

The process of going through any legal proceeding is complicated and a divorce is no exception. If you find you are at the discoveries stage, you are now beginning to understand why a cooperative divorce is so much better. You're also discovering why it costs an arm and a leg to get a divorce. All the rules and procedures that must be followed are designed to make the whole thing fair and rational, but slo-o-o-o-ow the whole thing down. Part of the objective is to have both parties disclose everything relevant to the case, so when a trial can't be avoided, no one has an unfair advantage in terms of having more information. And *discovery* is the process of lawyers learning everything they can about the other guy. The representative of each party has the right to question the other party under oath. An authorized reporter of the court is always present, to ensure that the questions asked and answers given are recorded accurately—they are evidence—in the event they're referred to at a later date. Answers helpful to the case can simply be *read* to the court at trial. Less obviously helpful answers can be used in cross-examination to verify or invalidate testimony. Those lawyers check everything you say and they watch you like a hawk. And if you step out of line with your answers—if your in-court responses don't jibe with your discovery answers—they jump all over you.

Unfortunately, it's not like all those American court dramas, and you can't simply say, "I refuse to answer…." You're obligated to answer any relevant question. Of course, not every answer to every question you're asked will be at your fingertips. If you don't know, or if you have to refer to your sources (tax returns, for example), you can offer an *undertaking,* or a promise to provide the answer later.

Pre-trial Hearing

Assuming you just can't settle this thing, the next step is the pre-trial hearing. Here, both you and your ex will be interviewed. A judge may preside, or a panel of lawyers may act as mediators. The issues pertinent to your trial will be rehashed, in the hope that the judge or panel can give you some knowledge and insight that will encourage you to settle out of court. It is at this point that people realize what this adversarial approach is costing them emotionally and financially. It can be a real eye-opener, particularly if more than one pre-trial hearing is held.

The Trial

Okay, so you weren't able to negotiate a settlement during the pre-trial and you're heading to court. The names of the players change slightly: whoever started the divorce—originally the petitioner—will now be referred to as the *plaintiff*. Now you're in court, here's what you can expect. First, each lawyer will offer opening statements, during which they'll tell the judge what they intend to prove during the trial. Then the plaintiff's lawyer delivers his or her case, followed by the respondent's case wherein the lawyer disputes almost everything and offers his or her own evidence. Both sides get to butt heads in the *rebuttal* and, finally, both sides sum up in their *closing arguments*. The judge makes the final decision in writing—days, weeks, or months later.

Preparing for court is an important part of ensuring you make a good impression. You can't over-prepare. You should re-read the discoveries transcripts, ask your lawyer lots of questions, and generally appear calm. Easy for me to say, right? Well, I've been to court—it is a little scary, but if you stick with the truth you'll be fine.

Dress nicely. Even in this day and age, how you look will make a difference. Wear a skirt. Believe it or not there are judges out there who don't like to see a lady in pants, and these are the guys in whose hands you're putting your life's decisions. Make sure you're on time, and leave your fury and gutter-mouth outside the courtroom. Don't raise your voice—remember you must appear calm even if you're seething inside—and address the judge appropriately. Try to look relaxed. Don't pick your fingers, twirl your hair, or jiggle your legs. Answer the question you're asked, no more. Don't elaborate. Just a simple answer will do. If your lawyer wants you to say more, he'll ask you another question. And too much information is deadly if you're answering the other lawyer's questions. Make sure you listen to the whole question before you start answering; in the interest of not saying too much, you need to know what the lawyer is asking you before you can answer. Speak clearly. Don't whisper, no matter how shy you are; you'll only be asked to repeat. Speak in an ordinary voice: don't be more formal than you would be in a business meeting; you don't want to sound like you're trying to bafflegab. And, for heaven's sake, tell the truth. If you're there for the wrong reasons, you will be found out. If you're thinking about making your case a little more convincing, forget it. Dishonesty in the courtroom is tantamount to the death of your case. Speak the truth, and speak it ever.

If You Are Leaving Him

It's not unusual for people to get themselves to lawyers and then, in the midst of the negotiation, decide to give it one more for the Gipper. Sometimes it works. Sometimes it doesn't. Several years ago a good friend of mine thought she had reached the end of her tether with her husband. A long time alcoholic, he put her through the wringer: debt, a merry-go-round of jobs, even a car accident. Finally she was going to give up and get a divorce. She contacted a lawyer, and had a separation agreement drawn and presented to him. He sobered up at the thought of losing her and, almost six years later, they're still together.

It's not so easy for everyone. After years of agonizing, counselling, promises, threats, and trial separations, it's same old, same old. There comes a point when you must bite the bullet and admit that your marriage is at an end. Unless you sever the ties that bind and go your separate ways, you'll never have a shot at the happiness you deserve.

But before you take the plunge, I suggest you do some housekeeping, so that once you finally call it quits you'll be ahead of the game during your negotiations. Slow and steady now, girl. Don't become so intoxicated with the future that you fail to strategically plan for what's ahead.

Step One: Find a lawyer. The world of family law is a relatively small one: everyone who's anyone knows everyone who's anyone. If you're not sure whether you're considering an appropriate lawyer, just ask another lawyer. She'll check with her peers and get back to you with the skinny on your prospective legal counsel. Don't know a lawyer? Ask a friend or family member to hook you into the system.

Step Two: Find out about the money. Don't announce your plans to end your marriage until you've gathered as much financial information as possible.

Carrie's Story

Jeff cheated on me just once too often. I was so embarrassed. There he was this forty-five-year-old man mooning over this twenty-year-old bimbo. He even took her to dinner at his partner's house one night when I was away on business. I was stunned when Cathy called to tell me that Jeff had brought the cow to dinner. What must people have thought of me? Well, I'd had it. I was determined to get my fair share and start over. I was a member of an investment club at the time, and on the pretext of having to do a net worth statement and retirement plan for one of our sessions, I had Jeff help me fill out a complete financial statement

Of course, you have as much right to the financial details of your family's life as your partner. Just tell him you feel foolish not having a handle the finances. If you've always been in the dark and it's the intention of your soon-to-be-ex-husband (STBE) to keep you there, you'll have to make like Sherlock Holmes.

- Make copies of all financial statements that you can find. This makes verifying information in your partner's financial disclosure easier. These may include
  - bank accounts
  - brokerage accounts
  - insurance—health, disability, life, property
  - pensions—employer's plans, deferred profit sharing plans
  - RRSPs or RRIFs, or individual pension plans (IPPs)
  - annuity statements
- Don't forget to look long and hard at the debt. What debts do you have and how much does it cost to pay these debts each month?
- If your family has used an electronic financial package such as Quicken, copy the file to a disk.
- Take copies of all past tax returns. These show depreciation schedules, capital gains and losses (which may identify securities being held), and the like.
- A copy of insurance-policy special riders can identify valuable collectibles that form part of your family's assets. Life insurance policies may have cash-value components that have built up over time.
- Copy wills, trust agreements, powers of attorney.
- Make copies of your STBE's last three months' pay stubs to show income and deductions. If your STBE has an employment contract, get a copy. You could also use his tax returns for information about his income. A self-employed spouse's tax return may not tell the full story, so you'll have to do a little detective work. Copy statements that show any other sources of income your STBE may have, including royalty statements, patent applications, license rights.
- Copy all credit-card statements. If you're responsible for paying the credit card off and he has an auxiliary card, consider cancelling your

account and opening a new one for you alone. At the very least reduce the spending limit.

- If you or your spouse recently completed a financial statement for a bank, get a copy of this statement.
- Do a household inventory using pictures or videos. Photograph everything.
- Take an inventory of the stuff inside the safety deposit box. Take a witness with you, and take pictures.
- If there was a pre- or post-nuptial agreement, make sure you have a copy, since the terms of these documents will affect the division of assets.
- If your partner has his own business, try to get your hands on copies of the corporate tax returns. Also, copy your STBE's expense accounts.
- Copy any document that shows ownership of chattels (cars, boats, etc.), real estate, or investments.
- List all the family's current debts, monthly payments, and reason for debts.
- Include any notes payable to or by you.
- List all assets in your name and your spouse's. Include whether the assets are held individually or jointly and the source of the assets—if they are inherited, gifted, or in the name of a third party on your behalf. Include whether the asset was acquired prior to or during your marriage.
- Make a list of all the issues for which you have been unable to uncover figures. For example, if your STBE has a pension plan at work, but you can't lay your hands on a statement, include *employer pension* on your list.

Step Three: Establish a financial identity if you do not have one. One of the most common mistakes women make, which they come to regret during a divorce, is their willingness to identify themselves as a financial appendage of their STBE. Women who have only joint accounts with their partners are a perfect example of this. The ex-husbands close the accounts, or empty the money out, and the women are left high and dry, with no way to buy next week's groceries. Or they have credit cards on their partner's accounts. He cuts off the account and she's left standing in the Zeller's check-out being told she can't buy her child a new snow-suit because her card has been terminated. It happens more often than women care to admit.

Every single woman should have accounts and credit records in her own name. If you haven't up till now, get to the bank and make an application. Having established your financial identity, you will be leaps ahead in terms of gaining control over your financial future.

- Go to a different bank (not just a different branch of your old bank) and open up a new account. This bank should not be in your home or work neighbourhood. I know it isn't particularly convenient, but you want to keep this account private until you've established yourself and are ready to make your move. Each week or month, take whatever money you've been able to siphon off and deposit it to this account.

- Get yourself a safety deposit box and keep copies of all your documen-tation in it.

- Apply for a credit card in your own name, because you're going to need a credit history. If you have never had credit in your own name before, you may still be able to get a credit card based on your "family" income. Use the card instead of cash to build up your credit history. Alternatively, you may have to use a secured credit card to establish one. (There's an explanation of how a secured credit card works on page 98.)

- Once you've established your financial identity, apply for a personal line of credit (PLC).

- Contact the credit bureau and get a copy of your credit report. If you plan to buy or rent a new home, your credit history will be checked, so make sure it's pristine. If it isn't, work to clear up any discrepancies.

Step Four: Find out how much you're worth in the job market. Been out for a while? Lots of women put aside their careers to care for husbands and children, never suspecting how at risk they'll be if divorce rears its ugly head. Time to get your skills up to speed. Think about a including a sum of money in your financial settlement for retraining or getting an off-track career back on track: money for tuition, books, and living expenses while attending school or bringing skills back up to date. A little knowledge and a fulfilling career can bolster your self-esteem and help you focus on the future. Has business been a little lacklustre lately? Keep meticulous records so no one can accuse you of deliberately reducing your income to negotiate a more favourable settlement.

Step Five: Find out how much it costs to run your household. Unless you know what the monthly costs are, you won't know how much money you'll need for child support or spousal support. If you're the one who pays the monthly bills, your job is easy. If not, look through a chequebook to find the expenses. Don't waste time being embarrassed at your ignorance; get with the program. The financial facts of life belong in every adult's repertoire of life knowledge.

Step Six: Put everything in working order, including yourself and the kids. Anything that needs to be repaired or replaced in the home, get it done now, particularly if it'll end up being yours at the end of the divorce. Take full advantage of your family insurance coverage. Have your teeth fixed, your eyes checked (get three pairs of glasses made, not just one), your bunions removed. Make sure the children are up-to-date on their dental, medical, and other health-related visits.

Step Seven: Stash away the cash. If you have no source of income of your own, it might make sense to delay your divorce until such time as you've built a healthy emergency fund. If your family is financially secure, but you have little or no access to cash, begin to build your inventory. Buy extra cleaning supplies, new shoes, and next season's wardrobe for the children. The objective here is to maximize your purchasing now, so you can minimize your costs once you are on your own.

Step Eight: Think about where you will live. If you're planning to move out, decide where you are going to live and figure out how much it will cost. Thinking about moving in with the new love of your life? How is your ex going to react? Haven't decided where you'll live yet? Look through the real estate advertisements to learn about rents. Consider what it will cost to move and calculate start-up expenses, including telephone and utility installation. Planning to stay in the house? Make sure you meet with your lawyer to find out your rights and what you can do to protect them once you've declared yourself.

Step Nine: Tell him. Oh, this is hard. Your instinct may be to blame him for the marriage's failure or for his own shortcomings. Don't. This is going to be hard enough for him to hear. Instead describe how the problems in your marriage have affected you. This is all about your unwillingness to maintain the status quo. Whatever feelings your spouse expresses, acknowledge them. And recognize that you'll be further ahead in terms of the emotional impact of your leaving. He may have to hear it many times before it finally sinks in that you want a divorce.

If He Left You

I am so sorry that you are living through this. So much is changing so quickly, I expect you're simply beside yourself, breathless with disbelief. If you think he may be coming back, I hope you get what you most want, but I want you to take and deep breath and hear what I'm about to say.

Whether or not he comes back, you need to get your life in hand. You may be a strong, capable woman who has always been in control. You may be a young, vibrant professional with everything going for you. You may be a soft, caring and dependent woman who feels she cannot cope. Whatever you're feeling now, you need to take some control over your life. I'm not suggesting that you rush through or deny the emotions you're currently feeling. But allowing your emotions to put the rest of your life, and perhaps your children's futures, in jeopardy is not an option.

Diana's Story

Initially when we split up, Justin told me that he wanted to end the marriage. I didn't really understand why. I knew we weren't communicating on the same level as we were when we first met but I really had no clue that he was actually thinking about leaving. We never really talked about that. It wasn't a complete shock, I mean I think I knew that there were problems. We were both sort of wrapped up in our own worlds, we weren't really talking about what was going on. Sometimes you go in separate ways and it's easier to talk to someone who doesn't know you than to talk to someone who has known you for a long time and has expectations about the way that it should be. He had met somebody. When he first told me that he wanted to separate, I couldn't understand what was going on, why now and why all of a sudden. I didn't want to rush through things. I asked him to go to counselling with me. He didn't want to go because he'd been thinking about this for about a year. He had met her about a year before.

I didn't know about getting a lawyer. I didn't know about any of that stuff. I really just wanted to get back together, to work on it. I didn't want to get divorced. One of my friends said, "I KNOW you should get a lawyer." My divorce hit me like ton of bricks. I was insecure, nervous, and emotional. I was sitting in the lawyer's office and I'd just get tears in my eyes.

To this day, I sometimes wonder if I'll ever meet someone who I'll ever laugh around as much. He was great, he was funny, he was neat, and he was volatile. About the divorce, he was aggressive because he wanted to get on with it.

The day that he could actually put in the papers for divorce, he did. He put it in that quickly. He's now married. It is just so weird. This is so not the way I expected my life to turn out. I never thought this was the way things would happen. I just can't believe it. But it is the way it is and sometimes bad things happen to good people. I think about people who have lost family or siblings or kids. This is nothing compared to that. I feel lucky that I don't have children. I talk to my family and my doctor a lot. I think people are surprised that the healing is taking so long because I tend to be a person who just gets on with things.

Step One: Get thee to a lawyer. You absolutely, positively, and without a doubt need professional advice. Get a good lawyer. I know how nice your mother's best friend's daughter's second husband is, but if he's not a fully experienced family lawyer, he's not for you. And I don't care how well attuned you are to your finances, if you aren't a lawyer, you don't have the expertise to deal with these legal changes on your own. And if you are a lawyer, you know you'll make your own worst client. So find a family lawyer—a lawyer with explicit expertise in family law—as soon as you can. Have I said it enough now? Let's move on.

Step Two: Find out about the money. Because this is coming as a surprise to you—sometimes even the most intuitive of us are taken off guard by the obvious—you may feel like you are running to catch up. But finding out about the money is an important part of getting a handle on your future. So go back and read the last section, "If You Are Leaving." Everything I said there goes for you, too.

Step Three: Get yourself some help in dealing with the shell shock. Some people use girlfriends. Some use a counsellor. You may be furious. You may be devastated. You'll need to talk. And if you have children, you'll need to find a way to deal with your emotions so that they don't overflow into your children's lives. This is very important. Take care of yourself emotionally (and physically, too).

Step Four: Take your time. No one else can set the agenda for your healing. Anyone who tells you to get over it is trying to help but has the sensitivity of a brick, so ignore them. You're the only one who knows how you feel. Try not to obsess, but do what you have to do to come to terms with what's happened. And give yourself plenty of time. You're the only one who can say when it's time to let go.

Step Five: Broaden your world. More and more people are recognizing that if you sit where you are and change nothing in your life, what you're left with is a life full of holes. This doesn't mean turning yourself into a whirling dervish of dating. But it does mean breaking some of your old routines, doing things differently, being open to new ideas. Accept your friends' invitations to dinner (and the blind date they've chosen to accompany the evening meal) with humour and a sense of adventure. Join a new club. Take up a new activity.

Step Six: Divorce rituals are becoming more popular as people recognize their value in bringing closure. Perhaps you want to write a letter to your ex, which of course you'll never post. Or maybe you like the impact of writing all the things that were not good in your life on small pieces of paper and setting them alight over a candle with Gloria Gaynor's "I Will Survive" as your accompaniment. Alternatives abound. Find one that's right for you, and use it to help you say good-bye.

You're Leaving Each Other

It's been estimated that about a third of divorces are cooperative. You've both decided that living together is no longer working for either of you, and you are planning to go your own way. While you'll still be sad, you'll mostly be focussed on bringing the joint relationship to a speedy end. Don't rush through the decisions and forget important issues.

If You Have Children

Saying that divorce can be very traumatic for children is at once a statement of the obvious and an understatement. Their lives will never again be the same. They will feel out of control, and responsible for the break-up, and they will suffer a huge sense of the loss of one or other of their parents. It is only in the rarest of cases that children are happy to see the back of a parent. Even parents who have been abusive verbally, emotionally, or physically still have a special place in their children's hearts.

When children perceive their family life to be disintegrating, they suffer a huge sense of loss in terms of security and sense of well-being. It is up to you and your ex to get your relationship to a point where you can work together for your children. You don't have to like each other a whole lot. You do have to be polite, friendly, and focussed on the kids. To get through difficult periods with her ex, my best girlfriend would mentally keep a picture of her daughter's face in front of her eyes. She said that made her focus on what was really important: her daughter's well-being.

Make sure your children know that they will always be loved and taken care of by both their parents, and that it's okay to love both parents. For heaven's sake, don't ask them to choose. Children need both their parents, so encourage their involvement and communication with the other parent and with other family members

If your child will now have two homes, it is important that each home be perceived as a special place. Terms like "real home" don't help to create a sense of connection with a new life. And kids should never be asked to comment on which home they love best. Don't criticize or judge your children's other home, and make sure your children have a special place in your home that belongs to them, even if it's just a section of a room.

In everything that you say and do, let your children know that you will always love them. Since children often lose their sense of balance when family dynamics change, it's important for them to know they are not at risk. At the top of a child's mind is the question, "If Mom and Dad can stop loving each other, can they stop loving me?" They won't arrive on their own at the conclusion you think is obvious. You need to explain that the love between a parent and a child is different than that between a husband and a wife, and that they will be loved no matter what.

Since children tend to blame themselves for the break-up of their families, you must also explicitly tell them that the divorce is not their fault. They will be looking for reasons for the divorce. And they'll find numerous examples of how they contributed to the family's demise. Over and over you must tell them the divorce is not their doing, and that you love them above all else. Help them to express their feelings. Listen to them. Don't judge them or try to talk them out of those feelings. Let them know that it's okay to feel sad, and let them know that you are always ready to talk.

If you walk around swearing at your ex, deriding him in front of the children, saying what a lousy son of a... —well, you get the drift—you'll be hurting your children. They see themselves quite literally as half mom and half dad. Tell them their dad is a so-and-so and that means they, too, must be part so-and-so. If you're so angry that you can't say anything positive about your ex, then say nothing at all. Ditto for remarks about extended family members and new step-relationships.

In the best of worlds, you'll come to a place where you can create and maintain a good working relationship with your ex. You'll be polite, respectful, and thoughtful, and you'll stay focussed on the best interests of your children. You won't make your children stand by and watch as you heatedly debate with your ex at the end of the driveway. Nor will you hurl insults, throw items, or scream obscenities. You'll accept that your relationship as partners has ended, but that your relationship as parents must continue for the sake of the children. So you'll keep the other parent advised about important stuff; you won't ask your child to do this for you. And you'll give your ex the information needed to show up for special events in your child's life, instead of insinuating that "Daddy forgot again." To this day, ten years after his divorce, my husband calls his children to remind them of special events in his ex-wife's life. He always gets a big "Thank you" from his kids, and he doesn't have to watch them be hurt because they forgot something important.

Above all else, let your children be children. As tempted as you may be to use a child as a source of emotional support, as your confidant, as your best friend, don't. She isn't; she's your child. You must protect her and preserve as much of her innocence as you can.

Spousal Support

Okay, so you've been married *forever* and you haven't worked in the past twenty years. Or you have been married for eight years, and you've spent the last four taking care of your babies, the youngest of which is just six months old. Or you've been married for three years, but last year you were involved in a terrible car accident and you haven't been able to work since.

Your husband has just left you. How will you cope financially? Welcome to the concept of spousal support. (Child support payments are separate from spousal support payments and are dealt with in the chapter, *For The Sake of the Children*.)

According to the Divorce Act, to determine the need and amount of spousal support awarded, courts look at how long you lived together (marriage is no longer a pre-requisite for spousal support), who did what during the marriage, and how much child support has been awarded. In awarding support, the court (or the lawyers negotiating) will want to take into account economic advantages or disadvantage resulting from the marriage's dissolution in order to alleviate any financial hardship that might result. However, the Act also specifically states that as far as is practical, the objective is also to promote the "economic self-sufficiency of each spouse within a reasonable period of time."

The determination of how much support and how long it should last is based on several factors including

- each person's current (and future) assets and income
- each person's contribution to the other's career development and education
- the dependent spouse's ability to support himself or herself, and the supporting spouse's ability to continue supporting the dependent spouse
- each person's age, physical and mental health
- the dependent spouse's standard of living during the relationship
- what it would take (costs and effort) for the dependent spouse to become independent
- each person's financial responsibility for another person (such as an elderly relative or child from a previous marriage)

Prior to a final order for support, a court may order interim support to tide you (as the dependent spouse) over until the final hearing. It doesn't usually provide for all the things that a final order for support would take into consideration, since this type of order tends to be made at the beginning of the process before the court has had an opportunity to hear both sides of the story.

In order to determine spousal support, both you and your ex are obliged to file a financial statement that contains a budget so that the court can see your total income and expenses. It is very important that this financial statement be as complete and accurate as possible, since it is the primary tool used in determining the ability of the payer to pay a support order and the need of the recipient for one.

Inevitably, the support order is always too high and too low. Payers who must now support two households (or some portion of a second household) consider the amount too high. Recipients who have been used to a higher standard of living think they're not getting enough. The fact is that, with a single pot to be split in more ways, it is inevitable that everyone will feel a little poorer.

Sometimes spousal support is awarded forever, or until the spouse remarries. Sometimes support is awarded for a specific period of time to allow for the dependent spouse to develop new skills or get on his or her way in a career. Sometimes the court feels that the payer or recipient could be using their skills and experience to obtain a better paying job than is now held, in which case the court will *impute* an income to that party even if it isn't actually being earned. Courts also look at your living arrangements. If they think a cohabiting partner is not picking up his or her fair share of the household tab, they may even take the third person's income or earning ability into consideration.

Getting a court to award you spousal support (and, for that matter, child support) is one thing. Getting your spouse to ante up regularly and on time is quite another. To help to offset the problem, all the provinces have initiated systems that remove the contact between spouses directly. In Ontario, for example, all orders for support, whether for children or for spouses, are registered with the Family Support Plan. Payments must be made to the Plan, which then sends the payment to the recipient. If there is any default, it is the Plan that tries to enforce it, although there are some circumstances where private enforcement is available.

But even these provincial systems have problems. Huge backlogs have meant that payments made have not been processed or forwarded for weeks at a time.

If your spouse threatens to declare bankruptcy, it's a scare tactic. Don't be bullied. It's just a negotiating ploy. Once you've received a support order, it is in no way affected by bankruptcy. While declaring bankruptcy will wipe out other debts, it does not negate a support obligation. In fact, your spouse's bankruptcy may actually work to your benefit since, having been released from other outstanding debts, he or she will have more money available for support.

The Legal Divorce versus Your Real Divorce

A legal divorce has only a few very basic concerns: to free you from the union of marriage, to divide your family property, to say who will take care of the kids, and to say who will pay for what and for how long. Most often, this stuff is negotiated and the law only steps in when you simply can't come to an agreement and must go to court for a judgement. All you get from your divorce is a piece of paper with the court's orders about property, custody, and support. From your lawyer you'll get a whopping bill. Now you figure it's all over, right?

If you think that a legal divorce will solve your problems, and that the judgement is the end of the whole matter, you're likely to be disappointed. Your real divorce is about ending one life and beginning another, and then making that new life work. It's about breaking old habits, and creating a new balance emotionally, practically, and spiritually. And it's about doing the best with what you've got.

Aside from the practical issues—how to get by financially, how to create a new parenting plan—your biggest challenge will be in dealing with the emotional fallout. Having broken the bonds that tie (or perhaps you're still gnawing at them), you must break old habits, establish new patterns, and end past dependencies. You must also let go of the anger, fear, guilt, hurt, blame, and resentment if you expect to move on.

And so we come to the next chapter, in which a divorcing woman learns that the emotional divorce may be one of the most difficult things she must ever do.

The Emotional
Divorce

After the death of a child and the death of a spouse, divorce ranks number three on the stress-factor scale. So there's good reason for feeling as you do.

Hit with the reality of divorce, you may be disoriented. It will sometimes feel like you're in a little red wagon careering down a hill out of control. You may be afraid. You may be angry. At other times, you'll have the sense that you are walking in slow motion through a thick mist. Your sense of loss may be huge, your sense of regret enormous. You will very likely grieve for the loss of your love. And if you're like just about every other woman going through divorce, you'll insist that you're just fine. Your denial will be gigantic, outsized only by the feeling that you are completely and utterly alone in the world.

Divorce brings home the truth of F. Scott Fitzgerald's definition of intelligence: the ability to hold two opposed ideas in the mind at the same time, and still retain the ability to function. While you may be feeling frustrated at your failure to make your marriage work, rage at your partner—or worse, rage at yourself—and desperation in terms of how you'll cope with the changes that are looming, you may also be filled with hope for a better life. In fact, the decision to separate in itself is a bold strike for optimism, since it indicates that you believe your life could be better.

Getting started with separating will be the toughest part. But other things will trigger the sadness and regret that comes with such a major life change. Even though I was the initiator of my second divorce—I've been married three times, which proves I'm an optimist—that didn't stop the holiday blahs from descending on me full force when December rolled around. I remember sitting alone in my new home, watching the snow fall and feeling incredibly alone. I love Christmas. It has always been a most magical time. But with my marriage over, with no one to make Christmas for, I was at a loss for what to do with myself. Turns out the big holidays are the busiest time for movie theatres, at least in big cities. All those lonely people are looking for something to do when they should be with the families they no longer have.

In her short story, "A Tale of Two Divorces," Anne Roiphe writes, "I felt as if the skin had been stripped from my body the first months after my divorce.... I felt as if I had to learn anew how to walk in the streets, how to set my face, how to plot a direction, how to love."[1]

Davida describes the discomfort she felt with her new title of "divorcee."

Davida's Story

It wasn't something I had chosen, and I resented having to deal with the prying eyes and the whispering. At once, I hated having to explain again and again what had happened, and I recognized how each time I told the story it became just a little easier. My mother had divorced and I carried the stigma she felt. I kept my wedding ring on to forestall any thought that I might be a single mother–you know, *unwed*. I was incredibly lonely and unwilling to admit to any other than my dearest friend just how lonely I was. I looked busy. I looked happy. I was miserable. The kids knew it, it turns out. They could hear me crying at night. But we never talked about it.

I know this can be painful. But I also know it doesn't have to last forever. Part of why we feel as we do about divorce is that we tend to think of it as a single event. Then we can't understand why it's taking *forever* to recover. The reality is that divorce is much more than a one-time announcement of the end of a marriage. Everything in your life is about to change, from your routines to your identity. You will have to build a new personal and social life. You will have to figure out new money patterns for your family. Your expectations will change and you'll likely also change your life goals.

Stages of the Emotional Divorce

Abigail Stewart's research shows there is a definite pattern to the process of divorce. It starts with a period of marital difficulty that results in the decision to separate. The legal process itself has a wide degree of associated conflict. Following this is a period in which coping with the day-to-day is complicated by a sense of loss or even helplessness. Struggling to master their new situations, women strive to become self-sufficient and competent. Within 18 months, a degree of emotional equilibrium is established.[2]

Elizabeth Kubler-Ross published a groundbreaking book in 1969 entitled *On Death and Dying* within which she identified the five phases most people go through when dealing with death. What's that got to do with divorce? Well, many of the experts who have to deal with divorce suggest that the same five stages apply since couples are experiencing the "death" of their relationship.

Stage One: Denial Whether you're the "leaver" or the "leavee," you'll go through a stage of denial. Kubler-Ross supposes that this period of "isolation" acts "as a buffer after the unexpected shocking news," allowing time to mobilize defenses and gather resources. Your disbelief in the end of your marriage is understandable. After all, how could something that, in the beginning, was marked by such ceremony and endowed with such hope be reduced to such bitterness and hostility? How could it be true that your family will be ruptured?

Since leavers have the benefit of being able to work through this stage long before their mates, this is a prime example of two people being at different stages in the loss process while going through the same divorce.

Ultimately, as the leaver, once you've worked through your denial, you'll file for divorce. But you shouldn't be surprised if, after the initial fervor, your aplomb is shattered. The first personal failure you experience—and, baby, it's only a matter of time—will send you into a nosedive of self-recriminations and self-doubt.

For those who have initiated the divorce, it is difficult to watch the agony of a partner who cannot seem to accept the decision. But you cannot leave a person and protect him from the problem; you can't be both problem and protector—it's against the rules. But the very least you owe your STBE (soon-to-be ex) is to be honest and forthright and direct. Tell him what went wrong and why you're leaving. Be as clear and concise as you can. Many leavees never get that, and are haunted by what went wrong for the rest of their lives. He will be sad. He will be hurt. He may respond defensively, with anger. Give him some time to catch up to you. If he never gets closure, it will make it more difficult for him to move on.

If you're the leavee, you will be further behind your already disengaged partner and you won't accept that something's gone wrong.

Alice's Story

I was so shocked when my ex walked out that I refused to see a lawyer. When it began to sink in, I had already refused to accept his first two offers. Finally my lawyer sat me down and said, "Wake up! You're going to blow this." I did wake up, but it was more like waking from a late afternoon nap than a good night's sleep. Everything was a little hazy, I didn't know where I was, and I was groggy for a long time.

Denial often also brings with it a sense of being overwhelmed. So many things to do. So many changes. How will you cope? The answer is *one problem at a time*. Of course, with so many changes to initiate or respond to, the first step will be to choose the problems that are the most important. Yes, I'm telling you to make a list and prioritize it.

I just couldn't keep my mind on anything. I kept thinking about the past, what a great life I had. I was afraid of making any decisions because they all seemed so permanent. If we sold the house, where would I live? If I decided to keep the house, but leave Mike's pension plan alone, would i have anything to live on when I got to be an old lady? Would the kids hate me for making them move to a new neighbourhood and school?

I was so worried it paralyzed me. I finally decided to go to a divorce group to get some help. I ended up making some great new friends there who could identify with what I was going through. One woman told me that she worried from 2:30 to 3:00 each afternoon. I laughed when I heard this, but she swore by it. She said if she saved up all her worry, wrote it down whenever it popped into her head and set it aside for her afternoon worry session, then she could get all her worrying done at once and it wouldn't foul up the rest of her day. I thought she was nuts at first. But when I tried it I found that those awful self-doubts, those questions that make you think you'll never make it, became less and less intrusive.

According to Buddhism, the ability to know your own thoughts, to be aware at all times of what you are thinking, is one of the roads to enlightenment. For years I've practised this. I'm not officially Buddhist, but I believe in this technique because I know it has changed my life. Before—when worry, stress, those dreadful thoughts that seem to just seep into my mind would take over, dampening my spirits, making me less of who I really was—I had no way to fight back. Once I learned to watch my thoughts, to be aware of where my mind was taking me, I learned to redirect it so that it went where I wanted to go. Some psychologists refer to this as "thought stoppage." They suggest wearing a rubber band around your wrist and snapping it each time you begin to worry. But I don't hold with that; I don't see the point of adding more pain to your already aching self. Of course, it's up to you to decide what will work best. Thought-watching doesn't come naturally or easily. It takes practice (but it doesn't hurt). In a relatively short time you'll begin to derive the benefits of being in control of your mind, as opposed to letting your mind take you down every back-alley in Worst Case Town.

The fact that you're unwilling to accept that a divorce is happening to you can also make you a difficult client for your lawyer to deal with. Unwilling to admit your marriage is ending, you may be more interested in your lawyer coming up with stalling tactics—to give your partner a chance to reconsider—than in negotiating a reasonable end.

Stage Two: Anger You're ticked off. Again, whether you're the leaver or the leavee, you will get angry. Leavers often are angry at their mate's unwillingness to do what was necessary to make things work. And if their mates come begging for a second chance, leavers become furious at the mate's inability to deal with the fact that they've blown it.

If you're the leavee, you're a little like a pinball machine: Every time something happens to touch a nerve, you light up and ring with temper. You're outraged. You're looking for someone to blame. You hate everyone: the other woman, the child who doesn't hate your ex as much as you do, the friends who sit on the fence—or worse, the friends who are on his side. You want to kill him.

Carrie's Story

After what he'd done, sneaking around behind my back like that, how could I face anyone? You know what I mean? I was so embarrassed. I called his partner and gave him an earful for being a party to Jeff's deceit. I called all our friends to try and find out who knew, who hadn't told me. When I found out that Jackie, the woman I thought was my best friend, also knew, I told her never to speak to me again. She said she couldn't tell me, that Jeff had been doing this forever. This wasn't the first affair. So all those people have been watching my life, snickering for years. I guess the wife is the last one to find out anything. We still don't speak, Jackie and me I mean. And sometimes I miss her. But how could she do that to me? How could any of them just stand by and watch him ruin my life, ruin our children's lives, and not say a word to me? Didn't I have a right to know?

If you try to instruct your lawyer while you're in a whirling fury, you'll likely do yourself more harm than good. Carrie reports having done herself and her children a disservice because she couldn't let go.

> I was so mad at him for leaving me for that young, gorgeous bimbo that I just wanted to punish him. How dare he walk out on me?! How dare he prove my life to be a lie? I worked hard for that life. And then it was gone. Had I just held my peace I would have come out with almost $80,000 more in cold, hard cash. As it was, my anger made my lawyer rich.

Your anger doesn't have to be self-defeating. You can invest it in rebuilding your life instead of in tearing down what is no longer yours anyway. It's a matter of recognizing where your anger comes from and dealing with it appropriately.

If what you're feeling is "hang-over" anger, the anger left over from all the things that went wrong with your marriage, you'll have to let go. There's nothing you can do to change the past. What's done is done. Talk it out, as long as talking doesn't incite you to riot. If raging aloud makes you angrier, you'll have to try something else. Fantasizing often gives as much gratification as actually carrying through with an act of revenge. So you could imagine burning his suits, setting his car on fire, pouring wine down his new girl's dress in a restaurant. Imagine whatever you want. Vividly create the whole story just as you would like it to happen. Keep it a fantasy, and you can have your sweet revenge without having to pay the price in terms of legal repercussions, regret, or guilt.

Stage Three: Bargaining   It's not uncommon for this stage to overlap slightly with the previous one. Since you may not want the marriage to end, you may be willing to give away the farm to keep it together. On the flip side, if you're the leaver and your mate is begging you to come back, you may feel all powerful. Resist the urge to be a jerk and take your ex for all he's worth. And don't think that, because he wants out of the marriage, you have the right to hold his children as ransom. The courts don't look kindly on it, and neither will your children when they eventually figure it all out.

Stage Four: Depression It is in this stage that you will likely experience your greatest sense of loss. You know what you had is gone—your family, your life partner, your best friend, your stuff, your home. You also know that what you could have had is also gone—the dreams you created together, the future you worked toward as a team, the shared joy of watching as a couple as your children grow. On all sides you feel you are the loser, so you no longer care what happens to you.

This is not the time to negotiate. Giving away the store because you see further fighting as pointless leaves you vulnerable in the future.

Alice's Story

I didn't care if I didn't get support. If it was all going to be over, what was I fighting for? Even the judge was surprised that I wasn't asking for support. He said, "You've been married for 18 years. You should have support." But I wouldn't take it. And when I ended up having to borrow from my parents just to keep food on the table for the kids, I realized what a fool I'd been.

Stage Five: Acceptance It's over. You've both got other lives. You're moving on. Now you can find other ways to fulfill the needs your ex used to satisfy in your life. You find you miss less and less of your old life.

Moving On

Even after you think you have gone through the worst of your loneliness and sadness, you may experience feelings of regret as you question whether you did the right thing. Missing your spouse's positive aspects is normal. Agonizing over the diminished time with your children is normal. And, whether or not you have kids, you may despair because you are older than you were and your life did not turn out the way you expected.

One way to help get yourself to acceptance is to actively work on replacing your married life with a satisfying single life. Start by recognizing the role your ex used to play and by looking for ways to fill the holes left by his absence. Make a list of the things he used to do that you miss, then try to find other ways to satisfy those needs. You can hire a gardener to cut the lawn. You can get yourself a good mechanic to take care of the car. You may have to take cooking lessons, learn to budget and invest your own money, or acquire other survival skills.

For women who have been in relationships for a long, long time, the end of their marriages sometimes brings a sense of rebirth. They have the opportunity to explore who they are and to take care of themselves first. This can feel like unbridled freedom when compared to the years of considering everyone else's needs, wants, and desires first. You are like the phoenix, rising out of the fires of divorce to be reborn stronger, more vital, and desirous of the opportunity to spread your wings and take flight on a new life.

While the emotional divorce will likely never keep pace with the legal proceedings—the leaver often is way ahead of the proceedings emotionally, while the leavee feels she is sprinting to catch up — the divorce will not be complete until you come to terms with the psychological ending. For some women this takes months, for others decades. But as long as you hold on to the bitterness, the negativity, the pain, you will remain in the divorce, unable to continue with your life.

When you finally come out the other side of your divorce, you'll be stronger. Of the 121 women who participated in Abigail Stewart's study, 70 percent said they felt that their personality had changed for the better; 38 percent felt more independent; 31 percent said they were happier; and 17 percent felt they were less stressed.[3]

Diana's Story

I believe that I've become a better person. I believe that I'm a lot more understanding. I started to really understand that different things were important to different people. And I started to learn a lot more about being compassionate. There have been many lessons. There are things I've learned about myself and things that I need to do to be a better partner to someone. I look forward to being able to receive love the way that I know that I can. A lot of people say that's what you deserve, you really deserve that. So I'm much better off without him. You want people to love you for who you are.

An Exercise

Here's a pen-and-paper exercise to help you look at your fears for the future and imagine your life, if you get a divorce and if you don't.

1. You were divorced two years ago. What does your life look like today? What are you doing? What are you feeling? Who are your friends? How have your children coped? What are they doing with friends? In school? What kind of relationship do you have with your former spouse? What's your former spouse's relationship with your children? Where is everyone living?

2. You did not divorce two years ago. You are still together. What does your life look like today? What are you doing? What are you feeling? Who are your friends? How have your children coped? What are they doing with friends? In school? What kind of relationship do you have with your spouse? What's your spouse's relationship with your children? Where is everyone living?

Fridge Notes

And here's a checklist for the front of your fridge to help you stay focussed on the positives:

Today I will...

❑ Laugh. It will help me to heal.

❑ Speak kindly to my friends no matter how nasty I feel.

❑ Be gentle with my children no matter how frustrated and tired I am.

❑ Say something nice about my ex, so I don't only say mean things.

❑ Stay busy volunteering or at work.

❑ Be assertive and clear in what I want.

❑ Be kind to myself, because I am growing and that takes courage.

New Roles, New Relationships

Alice's Story

When Tom left, not only did I lose my best friend, I lost my family. My parents died when I was in my teens and when I met Tom's family I fell in love with them too. They were loud, noisy, and full of fun. His mother is an angel, she was so kind to me, she took such good care of my children in those early years. When he walked out, she called to say she loved me. But I knew she loved her son more and that it would never again be the same. I see her from time to time, you know, when I drop the kids off for a visit, or when she pops over during the holidays to bring them treats. But Tom does birthdays and holidays with his family, and I have mine … two cats. I feel so alone sometimes.

It can be difficult to let go of family members you've acquired through marriage and have come to love. But it is virtually impossible to maintain the same kind of relationship with your STBE's family as you had while you were married. Mind you, some people do it. Against the odds, they carve out their own relationships and live those to the hilt. For the majority, though, divorce brings more than one poignant goodbye.

If you're determined to keep your extended family post-divorce, you'll have to make up the rules as you go. And you will likely have to brace yourself for times when you cannot be a part of the mix. If you cannot let go, you also have to ask yourself whether you are staying connected because you love those people, or because you want to retain any gossamer you can that links you to your STBE.

After my second husband and I divorced, I had nothing more to do with his family or friends. I just walked away. There were times when I missed my stepdaughter. But seeing her dad and having to deal with her mother would have been a strain for me. So I didn't. She has children now, and I often wonder what they look like. My ex also got custody of all his friends and I of mine. It's funny, through all the years, we had so few that were "ours."

You, too, may find your friends divvied up like so many alleys after a schoolyard fight. It is only in the rarest of cases that two exes can maintain their ties with the same close friends. Pals often feel they are being asked to choose sides, and so one or the other member of the couple inherits them. Often the friends themselves feel divided in their loyalties. Sometimes, one member of the couple will inherit all the friends.

Since divorce often brings new values, new directions, new goals—the very ties that bound you to old friends—finding new friends becomes almost mandatory. The changes in the way you choose to pursue life's pleasures, the new focus you place on things like health and education, leave you estranged from your old friends as it did from your old life. Some people worry that, since most of their friends are married, they will now be seen as the pariah, the gay divorcee, just looking for a man to nibble on. But this is often a projection on the part of the newly divorced, a myth.

Even sadder for the newly divorced is the idea that their ending relationship was a waste. I remember a girlfriend saying something to this end when my second marriage was over: Oh, what a waste of all those years. Of course, being the philosopher that I am, I never felt that way. But then again, who would ever want to have their life with another person erased just because it didn't last forever?

Building Bridges

When all hope of reconciliation has died, it is natural that what follows is a change of focus. Now you'll begin to think more about what this all means to *you*. This turning point is a dangerous one. As self-interest becomes your primary focus, you may be tempted to stop caring about your ex completely. You may even convince yourself that this is a healthy way to deal with the loss: "I do not want what I have not got." Whoa, girl. Move too quickly in this direction and you could find things going downhill fast. Selfishness, unwillingness to cooperate, and a desire to inflict pain may not be far behind. And allowing your relationship—yes, you still have a relationship— to become wholly antagonistic isn't in anyone's best interests.

That your ex was fifteen minutes late picking up or dropping off the kids is unimportant, so don't get your britches in a twist. And if he's early, that's no excuse to make him wait in the car until the witching hour. Just remember—everything that goes around comes around. And every piece of hurt, pain, thoughtlessness, disrespect, or disdain will revisit you in spades.

It's hard. I know it's hard. But you need to put yourself on a path of healing. That probably means finding someone to act as a sounding board. Friends, a therapist, or a support group can all work as outlets, helping you to get rid of the negative emotions. You could also run for your life—it's been long reported that physical activity is one of the best ways to deal with strong emotion. Some women have resorted to dart throwing, pictures of their exes pasted directly over the bull's eyes. But, while this is funny to think about, too much *him* and not enough *you* in your healing won't really get you to where you want to be. Weight training, on the other hand, will leave you too exhausted to obsess, and will and help protect you from osteoporosis!

Perhaps the most important thing, as you work to form a new relationship with your ex, is to recognize that there are two yous. There's the emotional you: the one who is hurt, sad, angry, frightened. And there's the logical you: the one who knows what to do to get yourself and your children through this with dignity and grace. Allow those feelings to co-exist. Deny your emotion and your logical self will take over, leaving you vulnerable to explosion when perhaps you can least deal with it, making you a ticking time bomb. Deny your logical self, and you are at the whim of how you *feel* today: up, down, crying for love lost, angry at how this could happen, saddened when you look in your children's eyes. Yet never resolved to make it better.

Ultimately, you must move from wanting to get even to wanting to get better. I've spoken with women who've been divorced for ten years or more and are still seething. Why waste all that energy on what has been? You have the opportunity to remake your life and for it to be something special, to make a difference in someone else's life again. If you've fixated on your role as victim—focussing on your suffering and misfortune, deriving your emotional satisfaction from friends' sympathy, stuck in the pain, anger, or loss—you've got to find a way to move through it. This was supposed to be a stage of your mourning process, not the rest of your life. It's time to look for ways to put yourself back on track. It's time to stop fighting with your ex and move to a new level.

The old relationship is gone and now you must redefine or build a new relationship with your ex. Initially, contact with him may be very hard. So there's nothing wrong with deciding ahead of time to limit how much contact you have. It is a truly strong woman who knows her own limits and works within them. Decide to restrict your contact to five minutes to begin. Over time, you can increase your exposure. If things get out of hand, you can always say, "Sorry, I can't deal with any more right now, let's pick it up another time," and skedaddle out of fury's way before the conversation disintegrates. Just keep repeating to yourself: "With grace and dignity, with grace and dignity."

Of course, neither grace nor dignity is particularly easy to come by. When you want to slam the phone down on him, your commitment to be constructive in your new relationship will stop you. And when murderous fantasies make your eyes glaze over while you watch him playing with his new wife and *your* children, you will refrain from striking out.

Instead, you'll develop a Parenting Protocol.

- *I'll speak to my ex as I would a business colleague or professional.* Before you next encounter your ex, hold the picture of a colleague or professional in your mind. Remember, grace and dignity. Make an appointment to discuss important issues, and be courteous and polite.

- *I will think before I act (or react).* In the best of all worlds, your ex will be working to help you, instead of aggravating you, pushing you to the edge to make you lose your cool. In the real world, your ex might be a complete jerk. That does not absolve you of responsibility to find a new way to communicate. Remember the children. No matter how upset you get, think before you act. Physiologically, when we're angry or frightened, our fight-or-flight response takes over; a basal response that helped us flee from enemies or fight to protect our young and ourselves. It has no place in your interactions with your ex. Here, you must defer to your logical self. Take a few deep breaths and give your body time to recover to a state of equilibrium. Think about what you want to say. Breathe. Think about how he'll respond. Breathe. Take the emotion out of it. Breathe.

- *My expectations for my relationship with my ex have changed.* Part of developing a new relationship with your ex will involve developing new expectations. If you're looking for friendship or approval from your ex, you're looking in the wrong place. You certainly wouldn't expect emotional support from your workplace relationships (close friends aside). That belongs in your private life, and your ex is no longer a part of that private life. Respect his privacy and expect that he'll respect yours. If it doesn't have to do with the children, it's none of his business. And unless a significant problem arises, don't interfere in his household.

- *When dealing with my ex, I'll focus on solutions.* Stick with your personal feelings about your ex and you're doomed. Be results-oriented, instead, and you can come up with plans that are workable. Remember, it's about the children—not about you and your ex anymore. Your marriage was about you as a couple. Your divorce is about doing right by your kids. Keep the baggage from your marriage in the closet. Don't keep rehashing the past.

- *My ex and I are a parenting team.* Many women try to take on all the parenting responsibility themselves. Those who had to do most of the parenting throughout the marriage see no reason why anything should change. Others may have had a shared parenting relationship throughout the marriage, but now that they're divorced they consider themselves primary parent. If you're one of these women, give your head a shake. Even if you have sole custody, you must consider the other parent's needs and thoughts on important issues. You cannot have a cooperative business relationship with your ex if you aren't prepared to play like a team member. Unilateral decisions will undermine your relationship and invite retaliation.

- *I will communicate with my ex as if he were my business partner.* You have a common goal: the children's growth and development. You likely have common financial issues. You're a partnership: not the old marriage partnership, a new parenting partnership. Now you have to learn to speak to each other in a cool, direct way. You must exchange information about the children, discuss solutions to problems, come up with action plans. You'll confirm your agreements in writing, including time, place, costs, and all other important details. You will keep the communication focussed on the issues.

Fridge Notes

❑ I accept responsibility for my own behaviour regardless of how my ex behaves.

❑ I will separate the emotion from the logic when I have to make a decision.

❑ I will not allow conflict with my ex to hurt my children.

❑ I accept that I was also to blame in my divorce, that this wasn't all his fault.

❑ Today, I will look at an issue from a perspective other than my own...maybe even his.

❑ I am willing to negotiate, to compromise, and to cooperate to resolve further conflict.

❑ I want to bring this relationship to a level where we can be fair and non-adversarial.

❑ I will focus on what my children need.

❑ I will keep my commitments and follow through on our agreements.

Conflict Management

There are reams written on conflict management. From how to bring peace to the world, to how to resolve disputes at work, to how to manage conflict at school—books, articles, and research abound. The funny thing is that, although we know that conflict is natural and that there are specific ways of dealing with it, when it comes to a divorce, the theory flies out the window to be replaced by screaming matches and death threats.

Whenever two people have a different way of looking at the same facts, or have to reconcile different goals and interests, there is a potential for conflict. While healthy conflict leads to solutions, unhealthy conflict occurs when we allow our negative emotions to displace our otherwise honest disagreement. Based on our past experience, our habits and our belief systems, and on how much they differ with our STBE's, the conflict can be minimal or it can be huge.

You and your STBE probably already have a predictable pattern of interaction that doesn't work. You have buttons that your ex knows how to push to get a rise out of you, and he has triggers you use to set him off and make him act and look like a fool. You're going to have to stop that. And you're going to have to create a verbal clue to get him to stop so you don't end up dancing on your emotional marionette wires.

Before you can get to conflict resolution, you must get past the emotional tangle, the war dance. You're the only person who can do this for you. That should be your focus. I'm not talking about denying your feelings; you don't want to turn into a time bomb, after all. But watch your feelings and learn to express them in a way that isn't destructive.

Active Listening

Assuming you've got yourself under control, there's always the other guy and his emotional smorgasbord. Tip number one: stay calm. Your first instinct will be to react—don't. Instead, encourage him to talk and listen carefully to what he's saying, then mirror what you've heard. *Active listening* is a great tool for getting him to calm down.

He: I can't stand it when you don't have the children ready on time when I come to pick them up. You have no respect for my time. You just love to keep me waiting in the driveway. You're on some kind of weird power trip. You: Okay, I can see you're upset. You think that, because the kids always are late getting out the door, I'm manipulating them to make them late so I can purposely keep you waiting, is that right?"

The "Okay, I can see you're upset" acknowledges the emotion and then the rest feeds back what you heard. If you heard wrong he has a chance to correct you. If you heard right, you'll probably get a "yeah" in acknowledgement.

Compromise

In order to resolve the conflict, you've got to create the circumstance in which both you and your STBE can win. It's called compromise and it's based on you each making concessions so that you both come out with something.

You: Gee, George, sometimes the kids lose track of the time and that's why they aren't ready. I try to get them to focus, but I'm always trying to get them to do stuff when they're doing other stuff they like, and I think they just stop listening to me. Why don't you call them fifteen minutes before you're due to arrive and give them a "head's up" that you'll soon be here. That might help, mightn't it?

A win/win approach means you both give credit to the importance of each other's goals. You want to get the kids out without being the nag; he wants the kids to be ready on time.

For this type of strategy to work, not only must you be tolerant of the differences between yourself and your ex, you must also recognize his feelings as legitimate (as he must yours). And you must both agree to play by the rules. Here are seven to follow.

1. You must agree that it's the right time to attempt to resolve a conflict. You should both have lots of energy—not be tired or angry. It's no good one person being ready when the other's exhausted. Make an appointment to resolve the conflict.

2. You must agree that the objective is to come to a positive solution. So you have to respect each other, and be prepared to forgive little sins.

3. Leave the artillery at home. Dropping bombs (unpleasant surprises) and using oversized weapons ("I'm calling my lawyer") won't contribute to a sense of mutual care—which you need if you're going to cooperate on solutions.

4. Focus on the problem—the specific issue or behaviour—not on the person's personality or motivation.

5. Don't rehash the past. Yes, he did all those things, but bringing them up now won't bring you any closer to a solution. And if you think you've earned the right because of all the rubbish you've put up with in the past, you've got to do some letting go. The present is all that counts in conflict resolution.

6. The Japanese believe very strongly in saving face. In the old days, samurai warriors would fall on their swords if they lost their self-respect. Help your ex to save face, and find ways to make sure you, too, don't lose face. Remember that this is all about win/win. If it looks like your discussion is going to turn into a battle, agree to call a time out, and resume again when tempers have cooled. Remember that *he who fights and runs away...*

6. You can't simply turn down a suggested solution. You must be willing and prepared to offer an alternative.

7. Having agreed on a solution, put it in writing. Then put it away. Unless the issue comes up again, it should be over. That being said, you should never agree to a settlement that you have reservations about or are unwilling to comply with. You can, of course, agree to try something new for a couple of weeks to see how it works.

If you want to use creative conflict management to move you to a new stage, you and your ex must be willing to work together. You must both acknowledge that conflict exists, and you must be willing to listen actively and communicate openly. Perhaps, most importantly, you must be willing to stay on issue, taking the emotion out of your communication so you can remain objective. You must negotiate, in a cooperative exercise in which you both win something. You must also be willing to make necessary adjustments and the appropriate commitment to make the solution you've come up with work.

Most people aren't able to totally eliminate conflict in their relationship with their exes. But you can decide that you're not going to waste your energy on fighting over lost causes. Of course, that means believing that finding a solution is in each individual's best interests. It also means acknowledging that conflict will do your children no good. For their sake, you need to find a way to make your new relationship with your ex work.

3

For the Sake of
the Children

Whenever I'm researching a new book, I become wholly involved, emotionally and intellectually, with the material. And when I began my research on the impact of divorce on children I got depressed, I'll tell you. According to the National Longitudinal Study on Children and Youth data, children are increasingly likely to experience parental separation at a younger age. One of five children born in 1987 and 1988 had experienced their parents separating before they reached the age of five. Current beliefs are that divorce is the worst thing that can happen to a child. As I stood on the school playground talking with other moms about writing a book on divorce, I was overwhelmed by divorce's negative implications for children. It seemed from all I was reading that, short of physical or emotional abuse, just about nothing justifies parents placing their beloved babies in the throes of divorce.

Thankfully, when I research I read everything I can get my hands on. So it was only a matter of time before I found research that suggests that many of the "wisdoms" of divorce are in fact myths. Imagine my relief.

There's no question that your divorce is going to change your kids' lives. But it doesn't have to damage your kids. If you handle it well, if you put the children first and foremost, they will come out of it okay. It really is up to you and your partner whether your children come away from this break in their family union totally traumatized or not.

Divorce is not the worst thing you can do to children. If you let your spirit die, your children will be hurt. If you allow yourself to drown in misery, your children will gasp for air. If you get drunk and stay drunk, hide in drugs—illicit or not—or consume your ex-husband's weight in pasta and potatoes, it will eat at your children's hearts. If you give in to the fear that you will have no money, that you cannot cope, that you are less without your partner, you will teach your children fear instead of hope. No, divorce isn't the only way to damage children. Sometimes it is the way to save them.

Studies have shown that up to 80 percent of women and 50 percent of men believe they were better off after divorce.[1] However, nothing in the research points to children experiencing that high a level of satisfaction after divorce. While children in homes where parents were desperately unhappy or in high conflict were relieved when parents parted, by no stretch of the imagination could researchers say that 80 percent of kids felt they were better off. But the myth that divorce is a catastrophe that leaves a trail of broken children in its wake is also way off the mark. In fact, research shows that children adjust to divorce in short order, reporting feeling less bad, identifying many positive aspects, and demonstrating fewer psychological and physical symptoms of distress.[2]

In fact, according to Abigail Stewart and her comrades in research, "there is every evidence that parents' well-being was strongly linked with children's, and there is considerable evidence in our data ... that the ending of an unhappy marriage initiates a period of personal growth and development that is good for [parents] and their children."[3]

A Kibosh on the Conflict

Davida's Story

I never realized the harm I was wreaking on my children until much later. I was so angry at Zac that I was determined to punish him. And since we had played the traditional roles—I as nurturing, always available, on-duty mom, and he as always absent, working, distant dad—I felt the children were mine. They were of my body. They were of my heart. I did everything I could to keep them away from him. He didn't have any right to them, and they were all I had left. I used my kids to manipulate him. I wanted him to beg me to see them. I rejoiced in saying no. And my heart soared when they pushed him away. But I've watched as my son and daughter have paid for my selfishness. When my son's marriage ended, I watched his child being kept from him, and I wept. My daughter can't seem to find someone she can love without reservation. She believes she won't have children.

As Barbara Whitehead puts it, "Divorce elicits bad behaviour, even among reasonably competent parents.... children may be placed at risk by their divorcing parents' bad behaviour."[4]

One of the most serious and most common burdens children face is the emotional tug of war that occurs when one or both parents try to get the child to side with them. Some parents may try to brainwash their children into seeing the other parent as the villain or as the sole cause of the family's problems. In this emotional war, the losers are the children who are caught in the middle. According to research, "Creating loyalty strains was the single most consistent predictor of worse adjustment for children."[5] The same research shows that parental conflict is especially harmful when the children are young (under nine in the research), or when the conflict is persistent or violent.

While conflict may be inevitable—you wouldn't be getting a divorce if everything was okey-dokey—conflict that manifests in terms of arguments and fighting are a choice. Couples who manage to contain their conflict, focussing instead on creating a new co-parenting relationship—those mature enough to let go of their frustration, anger, or disappointment—create an environment that is safe for their children. So while you may think your ex is a jerk, you do your children no service by saying so. And if you're venting for the sake of honesty or open communication with your children, you're fooling yourself. Your children have the right to a relationship with both their parents. They have the right to develop their own opinions. And it is not your job to manage their relationship with their father. *Anything you do that adds to conflict between your child and your ex you do for yourself, not for your child.*

Cooperation versus Alienation

No matter who you are—leaver or leavee—your divorce will be filled with a wide range of intense emotions, including rage, disappointment, hurt, and fear. But emotional ache does not have to translate into emotional act. An angry divorce is not necessarily an alienating one. Alienation occurs when you, or your spouse, choose to use your children to meet your own emotional needs. Perhaps you see them as vehicles to express or carry your intense emotions or as pawns you can manipulate to inflict retribution on the other. You can feel all the anger, dread, and fear of your emotional upheaval without acting it out. As a thinking human being, you have the ability—you must find the desire—to act in a constructive and cooperative way.

A cooperative divorce? Ha!

In a cooperative divorce, both parents work together to restructure their own relationship and their family so that their children will have as normal a relationship with each of them as possible. They recognize that it is the marriage that is over, not the family. This means cooperating with each other as to finances, logistics, and schedules, as well as actively supporting the children's emotional relationships with the other parent and the extended families.

Shauna's Story

Whenever Bob and I had to exchange the children it was often volatile. Finally we had to agree not to speak to each other. Bob would ring the doorbell and go back to the car. I'd send John and Jackie out while I stood behind the door and watched. It was so sorrowful to watch as this little four-year-old trotted down the path with his knapsack on his back, Tinky Winky clutched in his arms. Once

Jackie got in the car, she wouldn't look back at the house or wave or anything. John would plaster his nose against the window as his dad pulled away. There were times during those early years that I just wanted him dead so I could have my children to myself. I would cry as I walked around the house, lonely without my kids. Then when they got home I'd want to know all about what they did. Jackie clammed up when, after one of her weekends, I called Bob and raged about what the kids had been doing. Bob had let the kids go swimming even through John was having a wicked case of bronchitis. I was so furious. But Jackie even stopped calling me from Bob's place. And I couldn't call there because his new wife would have a bird and Jackie and Johnny would get the worst of it.

Some parents are completely unaware of their own emotional state or the effects of their alienating behaviour on their kids. And in cases where alienating behaviour is just borderline, identifying the behaviour can be difficult. See if you recognize yourself making any of these statements:

- You can visit your father whenever you want. That's up to you.
- It's no big deal if you miss one visit with your dad.
- No, I don't want to hear what you did at his house. What you do there isn't my business.
- I don't care if you do or don't go to your father's. Just tell me what you've decided.
- If you want to call your father, do it from another room.
- It was just a phone call. He'll call again. Why are you making such a fuss?
- No, I can't come to your hockey game if your father is going to be there.
- Tell your teacher we will need separate parent-teacher meetings.
- Hi honey, guess what? I just got a great job in (another province). We'll be moving in three weeks.

- I can't believe your father is having more children. See, you're replaceable too.
- Who do you want at your dance recital, me or your father?
- I'm not driving you to your fathers'. If you want to go, he'll have to get you and bring you home.
- How can you think about spending the holidays with him. I'll be all alone.
- So they're fighting a lot? That didn't take long. What are they fighting over?
- Here's a note for your father. I can't stand talking to him.
- So you had a great time. We have great times, too. Of course he has more money and a nicer house. But then he doesn't care what your life is like when you're here with me.
- Johnny, the phone's for you. It's him.
- Your father has to wait in the car for you.
- If he's late back with you once more, I'm going to teach him a lesson.
- Your dad just up and left as soon as you came along.
- He isn't very reliable, is he?
- I know your dad disappoints you a lot. He disappointed me a lot, too.

Cara's Story

Mom was so mad after Dad left. She stomped. She said he was irresponsible. She called his girlfriend, Doreen, all sorts of awful names. She said Doreen had stolen him. Then she cut all his pictures up. Anything with him and the family, she cut out his face and stuck in the picture of our dog, Luke. There wasn't a single picture of my dad left anywhere in our house.

Mom got very depressed around Christmas. She'd make me promise that I'd stay with her. I had to. I know my dad missed me, but my brother Frank was with him. And he had Doreen. He didn't need me as much. For the first year or so,

Mom wouldn't even let me stay over on the weekends. Dad had to pick me up and drop me off on the same day. So, even through he made me a nice room and I had stuff there, it wasn't really a home, just a place I visited my father.

When I did go to my dad's, I couldn't tell Mom anything about the visit. She said I couldn't even say his name. And she called Doreen "that woman." After a while it got so it wasn't worth the fights I had with Mom when I got home, so I just didn't say anything. Sometimes that would make her mad too. She kind of wanted to hear, so I'd tell her the stuff like the fights Dad and Doreen sometimes had.

I was always afraid that my parents would end up somewhere together and then the fight would break out. I never wanted Doreen anywhere near where Mom was. It was awful trying to keep them apart. So I'd just forget to tell Dad about stuff. If he asked, I begged him not to come so that Mom and he wouldn't fight. He was pretty cool about it, but I know now that he felt left out.

When the intense hatred of one parent by the other is blatant, the alienation becomes overt. Now the obsessively angry parent sees the other spouse as a danger to the children when no danger, in fact, exists. History is rewritten to emphasize the shortfalls and mistakes of the hated ex. All that was wrong is dredged up again and again. Reality disappears. Criticism becomes overt: "Your father never pays me for you on time. That's why you can't have those shoes." Children are identified as the victims of their parent's bad behaviour: "He didn't just leave me, he left you. How could any father just abandon his child like he did you?" They are asked to keep secrets. "It's just you and me now. We have to stick together. So don't go telling them anything about our lives together." And they are threatened with withdrawal of love if they don't deny the other parent. "If you really love me, you'll let your mother know that you'd rather be living here. This is where you're really happy, isn't it?"

Just in case I haven't said it clearly enough yet, here's the short story when it comes to conflict in your divorce. While you and your ex may be entangled in an emotional Gordian knot, you do not have the right to make life hell for your children. They do not want to be caught in the middle of a vicious fight. They don't want to be yelled at. The divorce isn't their fault. They don't want to be asked to choose. They love you both and they have a right to a relationship with both of you. They do not want to be overlooked. They wish to remain the centre of your universe.

As parents, both you and your ex have a responsibility to give your children what they need to be healthy and happy. You may be tempted to become mired in your own misery or hatred. And you have a right to your feelings as you work through this very difficult change in your life. But you do not have the right to inflict the stench of your decaying relationship on your children, to soil their relationship with their other parent or extended family, to spatter their lives with hurt and resentment as you drag yourself through the bog of your divorce. So, heads up. It is your obligation to keep your divorce and your parenting as separate issues.

Implications for Children

A study done by the American Academy of Pediatrics[6] in the early 1980s clinically describes the effects of divorce on children. Symptoms range from irritability, sleep problems, regression in toilet training, and separation anxiety for toddlers, to tantrums, hyper-aggressiveness, and poor school performance for older children. Pretty cloudy, huh? The golden lining is that most problems were noted as transitory. With appropriate intervention—helping children to understand the reasons for divorce, and aiding parents in finding outside support and help—these childhood issues are resolved.

The Academy followed up its work in the early '80s with a study done in 1994.[7] Here they reported that just under 50 percent of children manifest symptoms during the first year with significant reemergence on the special days in a child's life: holidays, school events, birthdays. For school-age boys, the biggest problem seemed to be aggression. For early- and mid-adolescent girls, the problem showed up as depression.

This is one of those areas for which a tonne of research has been done. While each child is unique—yours may not fit the pattern described to a T—here are some of the most common problems experienced and what you can do about them.

Preschoolers

Without the maturity and mental ability to understand what is going on, preschoolers often experience fear, confusion, and guilt. Look at it from the kid's perspective: if, as the most powerful figures in your child's life, you and your mate are unable to maintain the one relationship that matters most to your wee one, what hope does he or she have? And after all those little talks about patching up your differences, not fighting with friends and siblings, and "tomorrow is another day," your child may wonder why you seem unable (or is it unwilling?) to do whatever it takes to maintain the status quo.

The idea that parents love a child but not each other is a tough one to grasp. And since children are egocentric creatures, they often believe "mommy and daddy love each other because of me." The flip side, unfortunately, is mommy and daddy *don't* love each other because of me!

Preschoolers worry about the details: Who will take care of them? Will there be enough food? Enough money? Will they have a house to live in? Preschoolers' insecurities manifest in myriad ways: reclaiming a security blanket, regression in toilet training, increases in masturbation, disobedience, separation anxiety, and nightmares. They may fantasize about what has caused the disappearance of one parent. Their play may change, as their level of aggression increases.

And since preschoolers are empathic creatures, when they see their beloved mommy or daddy in a state of distress, they may hide their own upset so as not to be a burden.

In managing preschoolers through divorce, encourage them to talk about what they're afraid of and concerned about. Reassure them that they will be taken care of. Don't take for granted that they know both mommy and daddy love them; tell them. And try to explain, in as simple a way as possible, why the divorce occurred. Use storybooks to help explain that the problems are between the grown-ups, and that the children are in no way responsible for the breakup. Children often can deal with feelings by relating to characters in a story.

The very best thing you can do is stick to routines. It's hard when your whole life is changing to keep everything in your child's life on an even keel, but if you're always scrambling, if you're spending less time with your child, he or she will react. Try to slow down, take a deep breath, and stop for a cuddle. And if you can, let your child spend some time with other loving adults—grandparents, aunts and uncles, close friends—where they can be themselves and get lots of attention.

If a child does regress to outgrown behaviour, adjust your expectations. Whenever possible, simplify your daily schedule. Pay particular attention to basic needs such as sleep, meals, and exercise.

Let the family doctor, teachers and caregivers know about the changes in the family. They can best assist your children's adjustment if they have at least a basic understanding of the sources of stress in their lives.

Five- to Nine-Year-Olds

Young school-age children often respond to the news of divorce with grief. They miss the parent who has left the home tremendously, regardless of how great or awful the relationship was before the separation. In most cases, this is the father. In fact, very little negative emotion ends up being expressed about daddy, while mom gets showered in fury. If they do not have steady and frequent access to their off-site parent, they begin to believe that parent no longer loves them. Always there is the hope that someday there will be reconciliation.

Bedtime can be a tough time, since they may believe that, after tucking them in, the parent will leave during the night. Reassure them that you're not going anywhere. Being able to keep an object belonging to their other parent can help them focus on something concrete to lessen the distance.

Children who feel deprived tend to cling or ask for new possessions. Help them to deal with their sense of loss by keeping them busy. Sports, music and crafts can help focus their energies.

Just because you have a six-, seven- or eight-year-old who seems to be fine doesn't mean you're out of the woods. It may simply be that their strong sense of responsibility to take care of their parents is masking their own emotional needs.

Protect your children from your (and your ex's) anger and disappointment. Asking children to take sides is wrong. Never criticize the other parent in front of the children. And, most importantly, reassure the children that although mommy and daddy aren't living together, they both love their babies very much and will take very good care of them. It is crucial that children know —and they'll only know if you tell them and keep telling them—that even though one parent has a new home, they can be with that parent and can love that parent as much as they want to.

Nine- to Twelve-Year-Olds

Older elementary school-age children differ from younger children in their reactions to the divorce largely because they are more mature. With the ability to see the various points of view in a situation, these kids are able to understand some of the reasons for the divorce. But they do see things in black-and-white terms, and may feel the need to label one parent *good* and the other *bad*. In fact, some actually become an ally of one parent (usually the custodial parent) in the parental battle.

These later elementary school-age children are those most likely to bravely make the best of the situation. Highly sensitive to their on-site parent's emotions, these children are often also the ones most likely to hide their distress; i.e., saying that they see their dad enough, and that they don't feel rejected, when in fact they miss him terribly.

Children at this age may also become very angry. This is a natural outcome of the breakup of the family, but may also be because they see a double standard in the parents' behaviours. Children are great observers, and will resent their parents' inappropriate and sometimes selfish actions when they, themselves, are reprimanded for inappropriate or selfish behaviour.

Their identities, too, might be shaken. They can suffer significant amounts of stress, giving rise to a variety of physical complaints including infections, headaches, stomachaches, and asthma. In fact, pediatricians often report that these physical symptoms bring children of divorce to their offices far more often than children in intact families.

You've got to talk, talk, talk to your kids about the divorce, about what life will be like after the divorce, about how they are feeling and what you can do together to get through it. This age group is capable of understanding much of what's going on. Failure to follow through on agreements will make these children angry. Conflicts that take place within their presence will add to their sense of fear. Show that they have your permission to be with and love their other parent. Encourage them to call or write letters, help them to buy gifts, and don't forget Father's Day cards. Try to say nice things about your ex—this is the person with whom you had these children—and if you can't say anything nice, say nothing at all. Whatever you do, don't ask your children to take sides in your struggle with your ex. This is destructive and leads to more stress and even to resentment toward both you and your ex.

Someone outside the immediate family can be valuable in helping these kids deal with their anger and fear. Sometimes it's easier to talk with someone who isn't directly involved. Try to identify someone willing to spend time with your child, and include that person in family activities.

Thirteen- to Eighteen-Year-Olds

Being more developed, both socially and intellectually, means these children have more resources to use to deal with the change. They also tend to be much more focussed on their peer group than on the family. But that doesn't mean family isn't important and, unfortunately, one of the things this age group does lose is the relationship with the non-custodial parent, just at a time when they may most need support dealing with the social turmoil of adolescence.

If teenagers are left to their own devices, discipline erodes. It is not unusual for teenagers to act out their anger and frustration—everything from getting drunk or stoned to sleeping around. As if raising a teenager isn't hard enough for two parents, when the job is left to one there is less guidance, and children can be left feeling angry and lost. While divorce forces some teenagers to grow up more quickly and become more involved in family life, about one-third of teenagers become removed.

Since they are able to tolerate the ambiguities involved, encourage your teenagers to ask questions. Make sure your answers are honest and clear. State your own views first. Then try to explain your ex-partner's perspective as objectively and fairly as you can. (Yes, I know this will be hard. If he has run away with a woman half your age, you may not be able to think of a single good thing to say.) If you do not feel you can explain your ex's point-of-view, suggest that your teenager ask his other parent directly. Teenagers should not be pressured to choose sides. Perhaps most important is honesty. Since teenagers have hugely efficient b.s.-detectors, they will sniff out dishonesty, manipulation, and double standards.

While teenagers can assume greater family responsibilities, especially if there are younger children in the family, avoid relying on them a source of emotional support. Making children feel responsible for parental well-being and happiness can be a crippling experience during a time when they are busy exploring their own relationships.

Custody Issues

According to Statistics Canada, in each of 1994 and 1995, when there were 78,880 and 77,636 divorces in Canada respectively, more than 94,000 children were the subjects of custody orders. While the introduction of no-fault divorce in 1986 was intended to reduce divorce rates and remove acrimony, by 1987, just one year later, the rate had hit 44 percent, up from 8 percent 20 years earlier. The increase in the number of divorces led to the presence of a wide variety of living arrangements for Canadian children. The 1996 census shows that married couples with children made up 45 percent of all families; married couples without children, 29 percent; lone-parent families,

15 percent; common-law couples with children, 6 percent; and common-law couples without children made up the remaining 6 percent. In 1996, 15 percent of all children under 17 lived in lone-parent families headed by women, as compared to 2 percent in families headed by men.

Statistics Canada's 1995 report on divorce indicates that 11 percent of dependent children were placed in the custody of fathers, and 68 percent were placed in the custody of their mothers; the custody of a further 21 percent went to the parents jointly. Since these figures include only cases formalized by a court, they do not include arrangements that were not legally formalized as part of a divorce. So the 1995 Statistics Canada numbers on joint custody probably indicates a larger proportion of children in joint custody arrangements than is actually the case. As Statistics Canada reported in 1998, in the latest release of data from the National Longitudinal Study on Children and Youth, "most children (86 percent) lived with their mother after separation. Only 7 percent lived with their father, about 6 percent lived under a joint custody arrangement, and the remaining (less than 1 percent) lived under another type of custody agreement." This number seems to more accurately reflect the proportion of children living in an equally shared physical-custody arrangement.

When it comes to custody and access issues, it's important to know that courts are taking a strong position that the overriding consideration must be what is best for the child. Everything from the love, affection and emotional ties between the child and parents, to the length of time the child has lived in a stable home environment, to the proposed plans for the care and upbringing of the child are considered, along with myriad other issues including

- the physical and emotional well-being of the child
- the child's ethnic, ethical, and religious needs
- each parent's
  - plans for maintenance and education
  - financial position (to determine support)
  - moral and ethical standards

- sensitivity to and understanding of the child
- which parent is likely to to facilitate an ongoing relationship with both parents

Francine's Story

I thought that custody was a foregone conclusion. Patrick was seven, Melinda just three. I spent 24 hours a day with my kids. Melinda still slept with me. Danny just worked and worked. He couldn't take care of them. He didn't even really know them. He didn't know that Melinda liked her juice "not cold" or that Patrick was afraid of the dark. I told the lawyer and the judge to ask Patrick where he wanted to live. Was I ever shocked when Patrick said he wanted to live with his dad. I felt betrayed. I was angry. "Go live with your dad then," I said. But the court decided on joint custody for both kids. And I came to realize that Patrick wasn't rejecting me. He wanted to live with both his parents. He wanted what he had. He didn't want to choose. It was unfair to even ask him to do that.

Custody, *access*, *joint custody*, *sole custody*—the words mean so little to people who haven't been through a divorce with children. To those who feel like they have dragged their sweet little ones into a minefield, the words carry huge consequences. For some, the language itself is part of the problem since it promotes the negative connotations of *winner* and *loser*, and because it often carries a sense of ownership of the children. This inference of ownership not only sidetracks what is meant to be a child-centred focus—on the best interests of the child—it may fan the fires of what is often already an over-heated situation. Other jurisdictions have recognized the weight of the words, which are the fossils of a bygone era when children were the chattels of their fathers. In Australia, for example, the language of custody and access has been replaced with concepts and terms like "parental responsibility." In the United Kingdom the term of choice is "joint parental responsibility." In the U.S., some states have recognized the need to change the nomenclature and have come up with "shared parental responsibility," "residential placement," and "parenting functions." So it isn't a stretch that what is currently referred to as *access* in Canada be changed to "contact," "visitation," or "parenting time" as in other jurisdictions.

The difference between *custody* and *access* is the difference between being able to make decisions for your child, or being informed about those decisions. For years when custody was awarded to one parent—referred to as "sole custody"—the other was left out of all decisions affecting the child. Naturally, non-custodial parents thought this a travesty. They were not content with the visitation privileges granted through access: they wanted to share the responsibility for decisions being made about their children's upbringing, education, religious training, what have you. They fought for, and to a large degree have won, the right to joint custody. In this arrangement, both parents (and whoever else is involved in the case, such as grandparents) share the decision-making responsibility. If parents also have joint physical custody, the child will live in both homes for fixed periods of time. Some parents split the week, others operate on alternate-weeks schedules, and in some cases parents opt for alternating half-years or years.

Francine's Story

When the children first started going to Danny's, I had a really hard time letting go. They would be with me from Monday through to Friday afternoon. Danny would pick them up Friday at about 4:00 p.m. and bring them back after supper on Sunday. I missed them so much my heart ached. I couldn't sleep. I'd just wander from room to room smelling their stuff. I'd call every day, morning and night, and tell them how much I missed them.

I would send pages of instructions for how to do everything for the kids. When they would come home and tell me they had eaten McDonalds for two days straight, I'd flip. I'd call him and tell him what a horrible father he was. I couldn't believe he didn't have the good sense to put fruit and veggies in front of the kids, that he'd feed them chips and popcorn and pop. I hated it when they came home wired from all the sugar. It would take me three days to get them back into a normal routine and then he'd do it all over again.

One Sunday the kids came home all full of Danny and his new girlfriend. She had slept over and Melinda had gone and climbed into bed between them that morning. She really liked Karen. I saw red. Imagine the nerve. To have some woman sleeping over when he had the kids and then to let Lindy climb into bed with them. I considered going for sole custody at that point, but my lawyer said he didn't see much point. It would be a long and expensive fight and I probably wouldn't win.

While children are in the physical custody of a parent who has joint decision-making custody, the other parent doesn't have much to say—the custodial parent has all the decision-making power. And despite how much you hate the way your ex allows your children to eat junk, go without showers, or stay up late, as long as your child's health and happiness are not jeopardized, you'll have to accept the fact that at his house he has his rules and at your house you have yours.

Some parents believe that joint custody is awarded for the convenience of the parents. This couldn't be further from the truth. Remember, the system is designed to ensure "the best interests of the child" are met. So the goal of joint custody is to maintain the maximum level of contact with both parents.

Joint custody isn't easy. It demands a lot of cooperation between exes. And it demands flexibility. But if you truly have the best interests of your child at heart, joint custody executed without acrimony can be the best thing you can do to offset the implications of your divorce for your children.

Fewer and fewer parents are going through the circus of a full-fledged custody trial, with mediation successfully solving many custody and access issues. But some things can't be resolved by mediation, and sometimes this forces a parent back to the court system for a ruling. If you're contemplating this, make sure you have a healthy savings-account balance. Because custody battles can be very time consuming, not to mention messy, lawyers often ask for a hefty retainer.

Sharon's Story

I put up with a lot of Brent's nonsense over the first four years of our divorce. He'd change his days for seeing Jeff on a whim. Some days he'd bring Jeff home early without calling first. Luckily I was there. I often wonder if he'd just have left my seven-year-old on the porch if I hadn't been. Since Brent wouldn't speak to me—he wrote letters and left messages on my machine—we almost never communicated about our son. He had his rules—some seemed very arbitrary to me—and I had mine.

Then, when Jeff was eight, he was tested and we discovered a learning disability. That would mean a new school. But Brent wouldn't respond to any of my notes or messages about getting Jeff registered. Finally I had to ask the court to make an order for the registration so that Jeff wouldn't miss out. He was falling further behind academically, and it was affecting his self-esteem. It didn't help that Brent was on him about his schoolwork. Brent countered by seeking sole custody. He claimed that I wasn't pushing Jeff hard enough, that he wasn't learning disabled and that it was my fault he was doing badly in school. The court ordered psychological assessments of Brent, along with Jeff and myself. Brent, of course, was never available and the date was delayed over and over.

Finally the court awarded me sole custody. Brent still has all the visitation he used to, but it's funny because he doesn't spend anywhere as much time with Jeff as he used to. It's like since he lost the battle for custody, he doesn't really care anymore.

Fact is, courts loathe moving a child from the home of the parent who has *de facto* care and control. So whoever has custody when the interim application is made will usually retain custody until the trial. And unless it is not in the child's best interest to remain in the custody of that parent, interim custody often means final custody.

Child Support

Jurisdiction over family law matters is split between the federal and provincial governments. The federal Divorce Act sets out the rules for determining child support if you are already divorced or want to get divorced. The provincial Family Law Act applies if you have never been married, or are separated but have decided not to get divorced.

Remember those financial statements you were asked to fill out as part of the whole process of getting divorced? Well, this is one of the most important documents in determining how you and your ex will finance your children's upkeep, education—their very lives. Statistically, women have usually been the custodians of their children, earning sole custody in more than 70 percent of cases. Seventy percent of divorce cases with children also see child support being ordered.

However, just because custody and support seem to be almost a foregone conclusion, it doesn't mean that children are actually being well served: many support orders fell radically short of the amounts actually needed to keep children well fed, roofed, and in good health. It is this disparity between what it actually costs to raise a child and the orders for support that has contributed in large part to Canada's significant child-poverty problem.

Jen's Story

The girls were seven and four when Henry left. He just got up and left one day. The roof leaked. I wasn't working. Suddenly I had the whole responsibility. I was scared to death. He'd drop over and throw $20 or $50 on the table and say it was for the kids. As if it cost $50 a month to raise a child. Once we had a huge fight. I was yelling at him about how irresponsible he was. He threw the money on the floor and told me to pick it up if I wanted it. I was so ... I don't know. It was as if he wanted me to beg. Carrie walked over and picked up the money. She said, "Daddy, you shouldn't do that. It's not very polite." All I could do was cry.

After living like this for about a year and a half, I finally took him to court for child support. He had money. I knew he was working—building decks, renovating cottages—but everything he did was under the table. I couldn't prove his income, and the judge awarded me $50 for each of the girls a month. He told me my children were only worth $50 each. So much for the system. It did nothing for my girls. I've been working two jobs ever since to keep body and soul together. What's my option?

In 1997, Federal Child Support Guidelines were introduced (see Appendix C). "Guidelines" is a misnomer, since the formula used to determine child support is mandated when parents can't come to an agreement on their own. The formula was introduced to try and bring fairness and consistency to the amount of child support being ordered. It was also hoped that this formula would reduce the level of conflict between divorcing parties so divorces could be handled quickly and with less financial strain on the family as a whole.

The guidelines use a table of annual income ranges, which are matched against set monthly amounts depending on the number of children. The tables are used when the custodial or residential parent has custody for 60 percent or more of the time. (If custody is shared 50/50, the formula is adjusted.) The formula for determining the amount of child support under the Guidelines depends on three factors: income of the parent who pays support, the number of children entitled to support, and the province or territory in which the family members live.

Child support amounts vary from one province or territory to another because of differences in provincial and territorial tax rates. If parents live in different provinces, they would use the chart for the province where the paying parent lives. If the paying parent lives outside Canada, then you would use the chart for the province where the person receiving the money lives. The guidelines are very specific in determining income for the purposes of calculating child support. If the paying parent's income is from employment only, then his or her current gross income (that is, income before any deductions) is used. More complex rules apply for parents who are self-employed or who have more complicated forms of income. The Child Support Team, Department of Justice Canada, has developed a guide and workbooks to assist parents in getting through such issues.

Since the table amounts reflect average expenditures on children, and since some expenses do not lend themselves to averages, special expenses may be added to the table amounts if they are seen to be reasonable and necessary. These include things such as child-care expenses, including daycare or nanny expenses, post-secondary education expenses, "extraordinary" medical or health-related expenses, "extraordinary" private school, and other education-related extracurricular activities costs. I've put "extraordinary" in quotes because the courts are still debating what this word means. Judges consider what is in the child's best interests and how the proposed add-ons meet their needs, along with the reasonableness of the expense, taking into account parents' incomes and the family's pattern of spending before divorce.

So while the table amount will probably be the minimum amount awarded in child support, there may be circumstances in which the child support given will be higher. For example, when one spouse earns more than $150,000 a year, the amount of support is discretionary. The guidelines allow some flexibility about the amount of child support the tables provide so that circumstances in a particular family can be taken into account. Support can be increased or decreased if paying the amount in the schedule would cause undue hardship, and the household of the parent suffering undue hardship would have a lower standard of living than the other household. Let's say you and your husband have just split up and you have a whopping $35,000 in unpaid student loans. Since your unusually high debt relates to your earning a living—as opposed to resulting from a new world record for conspicuous consumption—this would qualify as undue hardship. Similarly, if one parent has high expenses relative to access (travel or accommodation expenses), that might affect the support order as well.

Since the guidelines were created to establish fairness in the system and to reduce conflict between divorcing parents, there is a rule for every exception. This makes the whole thing difficult to cover without boring you to death. However, if you have access to a telephone or the Internet, you can seek out information on the guidelines from sources that strive to make the whole thing less complicated. See the resource section at the end of the book for sources of information if you want to do more research on the guidelines and their impact on your family.

Mothers Who Work

If there's one area women have agonized over as they've moved from being primarily focussed on care-giving to become a financially contributing partner or sole provider, it is the impact of their working outside the home. As women, and as a society, we seem unable to come to grips with a woman's roles in the workplace and in the family. Studies abound that claim to prove that children are better off with stay-at-home mothers. Studies abound that claim to prove that children of working mothers are more independent, have higher self-esteem, and are better prepared for the future. It's little wonder that women don't know what to believe. And it's little wonder that women already fragile from divorce, who are forced or who choose to enter the workforce, twist themselves into knots at the mere thought of "abandoning" their children to daycare or, worse yet, a latch-key existence.

This debate is doing us way more harm than good. We're not resolving anything and we're punishing each other for choices we, as individuals, feel we have to make. After all, if we want to stay home and yet have to work to put a roof over our kids' heads, what's our choice? And if we feel stifled by not having adult challenges, close to losing our minds at another 24 hours of babbling, are we really better for our children as house-bound mothers than we would be balancing a career with our motherly duties?

The debate is moot and it should be put to rest. Women do what they have to do to survive financially and emotionally. My decision to work doesn't negate another woman's decision to focus totally on her children. And her decision to put her children before a career does not diminish my motherly worth because I choose to have both a career and a family.

How to Tell the Kids

This is one of the toughest jobs you'll have working through your divorce: telling the kids. Here I'm going to tell you what you should do and how you should do it. I know you may be angry, hurt, in denial, beside yourself with grief, suffering, tormented, lost. But, right now, this isn't about you. This is about being the mother of your children. And no matter how hard this is for you and your children's father, if you want to do your divorce right, at least for your precious babies, then you've got to get past yourself and focus on your children. This next part is about them. Forget how you're feeling. Forget that you'd like to kill the bastard. Forget that you just want out of this goddamn-hell-of-an-excuse-for-a-marriage. Keep those children's faces front and centre in your mind. Okay, here we go.

You and your spouse should tell the kids together. And unless the kids are of wildly disparate ages, you should tell them all at once. Working through this as a family will help to reassure your kids, and it will also help avoid their denial of the reality of the divorce. Even your very young children need a simple explanation. Telling them, and talking about it, will take time, so choose a time when you have lots of opportunity to respond, and a place that is safe and lets you freely express your emotion.

Encourage your children to ask questions and talk about their feelings. Reassure them that they won't hurt or anger you. Remain calm throughout. Cry. The pain of divorce is real, and if you don't hide your hurt your children will be more likely to express their deepest feelings.

As clearly as you can, explain why you are divorcing. Tell the truth, but without acrimony or blame. Keep your explanations simple.

Reassure your children that, while you and your spouse are divorcing each other, neither of you are divorcing the children. This is the area most likely to create anxiety for your wee ones. Change is always hard for kids. This rupture in your family structure will leave them spinning. Now, and for many months to come, they will need to be told again and again how much you both love and value them, that they continue to have two parents, and that it is wonderful that they love you both.

In cases where your spouse has made it clear that he will have nothing more to do with the kids, your reassurance is even more important. Help them to understand that he left because of the end of your relationship, not because of them and that his not wanting to be a part of their lives is more a reflection of what's wrong with him than of what's wrong with them. They aren't unlovable. They aren't deficient. And they aren't responsible for the divorce.

Of course, in reassuring your children you'll have to give them details of what their lives will look like moving forward: how they will be affected, where they will live and with whom, how their lives will be different. Kids will be particularly concerned about the parent who is leaving: Where will she live? How often will they see him? If you don't have all the details, reassure your children that, as soon as you do, you'll bring them up to speed.

Under the United Nations Convention on the Rights of the Child, Canada is obligated to move toward legislation and public policy that is really in the best interests of the child. In 1997, a Special Joint Committee on Child Custody and Access was struck to study the implications of divorce in Canada as they applied to parenting arrangements after divorce. This committee's many witnesses suggested the Convention mandate that children themselves play a stronger role in the decisions about where they will live and who will be responsible for them. In some cases, it was suggested that, for this to happen, children required "full, automatic legal representation and party status for every child whose parents divorce." Nice in theory but, given the weighted legal system and the pullback in government sponsored anything, this is a huge time-consuming and expensive alternative. Even provincial Child Advocates were quick to back-pedal from this responsibility, as current funding levels for child advocacy programs in Canada could not hope to cover the representation being suggested. Less financially onerous is the suggestion "a child's views, in an age-appropriate and sensitive way, would be solicited and made known to decision makers, whether parents, assessors or a judge." Perhaps even Auntie Barb, Nanny, or Uncle Greg would be able to provide this support and help to represent a child's interests in court. Of course this would have to be a bi-partisan family member, a truly rare critter in today's family jungle.

When the notion of using advocates is taken into account with the messages heard from the children themselves, it becomes clear that involving children in the decision is not only a smart move, it's necessary. According to the Committee, "If children are not given the opportunity to participate, if they feel that important decisions about their future are made without consulting them or considering their wishes, then children will not easily accept the decisions made about them." So if we don't ask them what they think, it may affect their ability to adapt to whatever custodial arrangement we come up with. The Committee recommends, therefore, that kids have the opportunity to "express their views to a skilled professional whose duty it would be to communicate those views to the judge making a parenting determination."

Of supreme importance in a system where children's opinions are sought is a sensitivity to the issue of asking kids to choose one parent over another. While you want your children to feel empowered, to be a part of the decision that will affect their lives for many years to come, it's equally important that they know they are not responsible for the final outcome—that they are not the decision makers. The issue isn't really the child's right to self-determination—which many children are not capable of—it is, rather, all about avoiding children's negative reactions when they feel arrangements have been imposed upon them without their consideration.

Of course, no matter how much you do to involve your children, no matter how mature they have been in listening to and accepting the divorce, and no matter how well you think your family is adjusting, don't believe what you see. Get ready for the backlash. It may not come as anger and screaming resentment. It may come, instead, as stomachaches or frequent illness. It may come as bullying and acting out at school. No matter how well you handle your divorce, your children will likely show some changed behaviour in the period 18 months to two years after your separation. If you can't see the change, don't assume everything is hunky-dory. And don't allow your desire to believe that your children are coping well to blind you to their distress. Accept the fact that life will be awful for your children and look for the signs: sleeplessness, heightened levels of frustration, a drop in self-confidence, increased dependency, lack of control or self-direction.

Keeping Daddy Around

There's no question that fathers' roles have been diminished as part of the divorce process. Not only have fathers left their children's households, they've often left their children's lives. Edward Kruk, a professor of social work at the University of British Columbia, has studied children and divorce for 20 years. He testified that a U.S. study shows that more than 50 percent of children lose contact with their non-custodial fathers. Using 1994 Canadian data—showing that of 47,667 children about whom there was a custody decision, 33,164 were placed in sole custody arrangements with their mother—Professor Kruk concluded that 16,582 of these children would eventually lose all contact with their fathers.

Children need both their parents. I know that often mothers feel they are indispensable. As primary caregivers, mothers may spend more time nurturing and caring for their children. But that in no way diminishes their children's need for a relationship with their fathers.

For decades, courts often applied the "tender years" doctrine, which held that mothers were generally entitled to custody of children from birth to age seven, after which time the father became entitled to custody. Since the mid-'70s, it has been the "best interests of the child" doctrine. Although the tender years doctrine is no longer part of current family law or case law, many people believe that judges still operate on the presumption that mothers are better parents. Yet there is no evidence to support the idea that one sex has innately superior parenting abilities.

The quality of the relationship is the determining factor in terms of any relationship being good or not so good for children. However, while an emotionally close relationship with dad has been found to be good for children, regularity and frequency may not always signal *good*.

Here's something you may not know. The United Nations General Assembly opened the Convention on the Rights of the Child for signature on November 20, 1989. Canada signed on May 28, 1990. After the requisite 30 nations had ratified the Convention, it came into force on September 2, 1990. Canada ratified it in December 1991 and submitted its initial report to the UN Committee on the Rights of the Child in June

1994. This Convention, which is the most widely ratified human rights treaty in history, sets minimum legal and moral standards for the protection of children's human rights. These include civil rights and freedoms, rights related to the provision of optimal conditions for growth and development (health care, education, economic security, and recreation), and the right to protection from abuse, exploitation, neglect, and unnecessary harm. The Convention expressly recognizes the special role of the family in the nurture of the child. A key provision of the Convention states that in all actions concerning children, the best interests of the child shall be a primary consideration. The Convention also seeks to give children the right to contact with both parents if separated from one of them, and the opportunity to express their views freely in matters affecting them.[8]

Typically, custody and access battles rage over who will get the kids, who will be in charge of making the major decisions, who will decide when and how often the children see the other parent. In all of these fights, it is never about what the children want. If an infant could speak, she would tell you that she wants both a mommy and a daddy. (Again, I am not taking about cases where abuse is an issue.) Parents' anger with each other, their desire to hurt each other, and their efforts to shore up their own financial and political position all contribute to the battle for the children. And the people who lose out big time are the kids. Don't do this to your children. They deserve to have both parents.

If there is a single good reason for working toward a good divorce, it is the children. While being consumed with rage, fear, and hatred may seem like the natural state of being during divorce, uncontrolled and destructive divorce behaviour leads to severe negative consequences for the children. Study after study has been done to determine the impact of divorce on children. The answer that keeps coming back is that divorce is a risky business for kids. They lose out on income. They lose out on connections with their parents and their extended family. They lose out on residential stability. Yep, they lose out. As a result they drop out—of school, of social circles, sometimes out of their families.

A Parenting Plan

A parenting plan is a formal statement of how the needs of children are going to be met after divorce. Hot in the U.S., these plans are attracting increasing attention all over the world as courts emphasize and encourage joint parental responsibility. Typical parent plans cover issues such as

- residential and child-care arrangements
- time spent with each parent and the extended family
- financial arrangements
- recreation and holiday arrangements
- resolution of conflict
- education and religion

One reason parenting plans are becoming increasingly popular is that it's now generally accepted that custody arrangements established immediately after a separation are hard to adjust. And since everything about the child's new life is, in fact, new, a formal plan made without the benefit of evolution will likely satisfy no one's needs. Spelling out social, medical, and educational implications for children in a formal custody agreement assumes you already know all the quirks of your child's life before he or she has lived it. In trying to decide who is going to do what and when, who will pay for the various expenses that come with child rearing, and how time will be shared, parents are acting as omnipotent creators of their children's lives. What used to be organic in terms of how parents made decisions about their children is, through the divorce process, being forced to fit a model that may end up suiting no one.

Here are ideas for areas that you may wish to discuss and resolve for your parenting plan:

- Who the children will live with (days of the week, time of pick-up and drop-off) by day, including after-school provisions and weekends
- Vacation schedule for winter, spring, and summer vacations

- Holiday schedule for
  - New Year's eve and New Year's day
  - Easter
  - May 24th
  - July 1st
  - August 1st
  - Thanksgiving
  - Remembrance day
  - Christmas eve and Christmas day
  - religious holidays
  - professional development days
- Schedule for special occasions:
  - Mother's Day
  - Father's Day
  - mother's birthday
  - father's birthday
  - paternal family days (grandparents' birthdays, etc.)
  - maternal family days
  - children's birthdays
- Day-to-day decision making
- Major decisions
  - education
  - non-emergency health care
  - religious upbringing
- Dispute resolution
  - who will be involved
  - who will pay

Working together on a plan, parents' communication can evolve from an intimate to a business relationship. Since no one else understands your children as you do, no one else is in as good a position as you are to anticipate their needs. The parenting plan not only establishes ground rules, but also creates the impetus for both parents sticking to the plan, since the plan acts as a tiebreaker when you disagree.

A Final Word on the Subject

One of the most difficult parts of being divorced from your ex, as it relates to your children, is the fact that you have lost your right to give him a piece of your mind when he disappoints, hurts, or saddens your children. While as long as you were married you could tell him quietly or loudly when he was stepping out of bounds, now that you're not, you are no longer entitled to speak your mind when it comes to how he's raising his children. That's his business.

I've watched first hand as many a friend has sought to manage the relationships their children have with their other parent. It's an impossible task, simply an exercise in frustration. The reason it never works is that the only people who have control over their relationship are the people directly involved. So the only person responsible for your ex's relationship with his children is your ex. If he chooses to disappoint them by not showing up for the school play, you don't have to make excuses; he just didn't come. You can express empathy with your child's disappointment, as in "I'm sorry you're disappointed, honey." But you don't have to sugar coat his absence to save your child's feelings. It won't work anyway, so save yourself the trouble. Just as important is the fact that the only person responsible for your son's or daughter's relationship with their father is your son or daughter. So if your daughter is going through a particularly sour period, it's not your responsibility to explain her behaviour. He's her father. He'll have to figure it out. Just like you did.

Ultimately, the only people we have any true control over are ourselves, and the only relationships which are ours to manage are our own. Don't bother taking on the role of Manager of Expectations, Director of

Disappointment-Assuaging, or Mediator. Your job is to manage your relationship with your children to the best of your ability. If your ex keeps messing up, your kids will figure out how to deal with him in good time. You don't have to balm their bruises or stoke their fires. And if your children are going through a period where they hate your ex, you don't have to make excuses. They'll go through stages where they hate you, too. That's just part of being a parent.

4

Women, Divorce, and the Money

Bernadette's Story

I was completely independent of my husband financially. I had a great job, built my own RRSPs, had a pretty healthy investment portfolio and my own credit history. Mathew was a moron about money and I got tired of always bailing him out when he got himself into trouble financially. When I finally left him, he got way more of my money than he should have. It didn't seem fair. I had paid off one bill after another all through our marriage and now he was asking for half my RRSPs.

When a marriage disintegrates, ultimately the question becomes "who gets what?" The division of property is governed by provincial law and therefore varies from one province to another. This is one reason why women seeking divorce must rely heavily on the specialized legal advice of a family lawyer when it comes to making a financial claim.

While the rules vary from province to province, the goal remains the same regardless of where you live. That goal: to divide the value of the assets accumulated throughout the marriage between the individuals.

Traditionally, women have been on the receiving end of marriage settlements. Having often supported spouses through their education and subsequent ladder climbing, having stayed home to mind the babies, women who see their marriages end are often compensated financially, as if money can make the hurt go away. But with the new independent woman earning and managing her own money, we're seeing the tables turned.

Diana's Story

What's interesting about the whole thing is that when Justin finished his MBA, he started to earn a lot of money and in his first year he had a very good income. I had a very stable income, had really started to come along nicely. I have stock options and things like that. Justin had just started to make big bonuses based on his commissions and what he was selling. What was ironic about it was that when it came time for the divorce, I actually had more wealth than he did. I had more assets. I had to buy him out of the house. It was really difficult because I had helped him get through university. When he went back to MBA-school, we owned a home and had a mortgage. I had to carry the mortgage by myself for a year. It was tough. There were months when I wasn't sure I was even going to make it. So it was ironic that when we split up and he was making the higher income, he still wanted things from the home. He wanted to make sure he got his fair share. We went through the process, wound up splitting the assets and I wound up having to buy him out of the house.

My lawyer said to me that I really did have a case and that I could have gone to court and pressed for more because of the fact that I had put him through school. But the only people that end up making anything are the lawyers. I didn't like the fact that I had to give him money when he was leaving. But at the same time, I knew that it would get me off the hook, that he wouldn't be constantly feeling like I took advantage of him. That was the right thing to do and the fair thing to do. What I'm saying is I don't want to be a victim and I'm in control now and it's up to me.

The definition of property—the stuff to be split between the exes— varies provincially. While some provinces draw a distinction between non-family and family assets, others do not. Family assets are usually made up of the stuff used by the family: the car, the house, the joint accounts. Non-family assets tend to be the things that the family didn't have much to do with: perhaps a business or an inheritance.

When it comes time to divide the property, it is the net value of the property (the value of the property less any debts against it) that is used in the calculations. So if you own a house worth $300,000 and you have a mortgage for $120,000, the net value of the house is $180,000. It is this net value to which you are entitled a portion.

In Ontario, the Family Law Act governs how couples deal with property upon separation and divorce. When spouses in Ontario separate, there is no division of property. What's his is his, what's yours is yours. However, there is a calculation made to determine how much money the person whose net asset value has increased most during the marriage should pay to the other, so that they each end up with assets of equal value. This payment is called an equalization payment.

In essence, everything you owe and own are valued for the date you got married and the date you separated. You then subtract the net value of the things you brought into the marriage from the net value of the things you owned at separation date (unless you got them during marriage as a gift or inheritance) and you'll end up with your Net Family Property (NFP). Then figure out your spouse's NFP, deduct the lower NFP from the higher one and divide the difference in half. That's the amount of the equalization payment made by the richer to the poorer party, so you both end up with the same amount—sometimes.

As with any rule, there are always exceptions, so you might, in fact, not end up dead even. If, for example, you received a gift or inheritance during your marriage, it'll be excluded from the NFP calculation, provided the money was not included in the matrimonial home. If it was used to buy the matrimonial home, pay down the mortgage, renovate—anything to do with the matrimonial home—the inheritance or gift will have lost it's protective shield. There are other exclusions and special rules setting out when you can or cannot deduct the value of the matrimonial home in your name, so a lawyer well-versed in family law is a must.

The stuff that isn't divided is referred to as *exempt property* and, again, the list varies provincially. Typically the list includes

- assets owned before the marriage

- assets exempted under a marriage contract

- assets accumulated after the date of separation

- gifts, inheritances received during a marriage, and family heirlooms

- items of exclusive personal value

- business assets

- gifts from one spouse to another

- proceeds from a life-insurance policy

- personal injury settlements or court awards

- traceable property

This last one can be a little complicated and speaks to the need to keep meticulous financial records all through a marriage. If the property started out as exempt property but ended up in another form, the property remains exempt even in its new form. So lets say your mother left you $40,000 which you put into a GIC; while the GIC wouldn't normally be exempt, because it came from an inheritance, that property will be exempted as long as you can show the paper trail.

Of course, the next question that arises is, "How is the value of the property determined?" This can be a very complicated issue, particularly in provinces that do not specify the value to be used. Naturally, wildly different numbers can be created if the value is based on current market value or book value (the value of the property when it was acquired). Add in the twists of whether or not tax and other financial obligations should be calculated, and what you have is a very windy road.

Valuing Pension Assets

When the asset being valued is a pension, valuation can become particularly tricky. If your province considers the pension to be a family asset, it must be valued and divided like other family assets. This can be a phenomenally complicated, and often expensive, task. Since the amount to be divided must only be the amount accumulated during the marriage, the entire pension will very likely not be split. Valuators and accountants must then be brought in to consider the method of calculation, mortality tables, early retirement provisions, death benefits, and tax consequences.

Just because evaluating a company pension plan can be an icky and expensive job, don't just let the whole pension thing slip away unnoticed. Chances are that pension is worth more than you think. Many people believe it to be worth only the value of the contributions made. Not so. Don't ignore this potentially very important asset.

You may also be entitled to divide Canada Pension Plan (CPP) credits equally with your ex, whether you're married formally or had a common-law relationship. And the fact that you're in a new relationship doesn't affect your ability to request a credit split for the period you lived with a former spouse.

If you were legally married and lived together for at least 12 consecutive months, and your marriage has ended in divorce or legal annulment, there is no time limit to initiate credit splitting. If you are still at the separation stage, before you can split CPP credits, you must be separated for at least 12 consecutive months. Either you or your spouse can apply to Human Resources Development Canada (HRDC) to initiate credit splitting. There is no time limit, except if your ex dies, in which case the application must be made within three years of his death. If you've been in a common-law relationship, the rules are the same as for couples who have separated, except that you must make your claim within four years of separation.

Here's how CPP credit splitting works. The credits of both spouses are added together, for the time they lived together and the total number of credits is divided equally between them.

These credits are not actually paid. They are used to determine the amount of any CPP benefits to which you may be entitled.

To apply for credit splitting, you must provide originals or certified copies of marriage certificate, proof of divorce or legal annulment court documents, and any separation agreements and/or Minutes of Settlement between you and your former spouse. In the case of a common-law relationship, you'll be asked to make a Statutory Declaration to establish the length of a common-law relationship. This declaration may be taken at an HRDC office at no cost to you.

You should be aware of a recent court ruling if you enter into a discussion about splitting pension assets. In the past, a spouse whose pension assets were being divided, and who subsequently declared bankruptcy, could see the payments to the receiving spouse decreased or even stopped by the bankruptcy. However, an April 14, 2000, ruling in Ontario's Superior Court of Justice in Ottawa made it clear that, if the judge ordering the pension equalization payments "impresses them with a trust," the debt will survive the bankruptcy process. The "impresses them with a trust" lingo is simply judicial speak for segregating the funds so they are not subject to other claims. The bottom line: if you're splitting pension assets with your STBE, make sure the judge rules that the funds are impressed with a trust (or, if you don't go to court, your separation agreement is worded accordingly) so if the worst does happen you won't be left out in the cold.

Negotiating a Settlement

Often women choose to keep the family home, giving up retirement assets in exchange. But this isn't always a smart move. But women who have stayed out of the work force to raise a family, or who have lower paying jobs, need to hold on to at least a portion of the family's retirement assets. With no RRSP room to catch up, you'll be starting from ground zero if you relinquish RRSP assets totally. This is particularly important if you are in your late forties or fifties and have less time to rebuild a strong retirement asset base.

A fifty-fifty split of RRSP assets may seem fair, but if your spouse also has a company pension plan, that has to be taken into consideration. If you won't be entering the work force immediately, you'll need to negotiate extra income for investment purposes so you don't spend several years contributing zilch to your retirement plan. Also keep in mind that if your spouse has significant unused RRSP contribution room—if he could have made contributions but chose not to—those catch-up contributions aren't divisible after the settlement. Negotiate for a portion of those contributions to be made in your name (as a spousal contribution) prior to the division of assets, and that the spousal RRSP will not be equalized. That way you'll have assets that can continue to grow on a tax deferred basis.

Once you are living separately, the RRSP rules for withdrawals from a spousal plan change. The money will be taxed in your hands, so don't go grabbing money out of your spousal plan thinking your old buddy will get stuck with the tax bill. You'll end up paying the piper.

Most people don't even know what contingent liabilities are, let alone take them into account when figuring out how to split their assets. A contingent liability is a liability that has yet to rear its ugly head. It's something that you may owe in the future, like taxes, fees, or other expenses. A perfect example of this is a case where registered and non-registered assets are being equalized separately—let's say one person is taking the RRSP and the other is taking the house. There has to be some recognition that the party holding the RRSP will be taxed when those funds are withdrawn, so the RRSP holder negotiates that those assets be discounted for the tax that will be paid on them. The same kind of negotiation would protect the spouse who took the house as settlement if that house had to be sold a short while down the road. Factoring in the reduction in the asset for legal fees, real estate commission, GST, and incidental expenses evens the playing field in terms of income after taxes and expenses.

Worried about the tax you might have to pay because an asset you're assuming has a contingent tax liability? You can choose not to have income attribution rules for capital gains apply to you by formally filing an election at the next tax filing after the split of assets. For example, Jane takes over an asset such as a painting that is subject to capital gains tax, and the painting goes up in value. If it's sold within the next year, the tax man would want to tax only her ex-husband, John. By filing the election, the asset would be taxed in Jane's hands, where the tax owed would be lower.

The Matrimonial Home

The one asset that doesn't get lumped in under the categories we've looked at so far is the matrimonial home. The matrimonial home is any residence in which either party has a legal interest (so that applies to the home you own or rent) which is ordinarily occupied by the spouses as their family residence at separation or immediately before separation. If you have a city house that you ordinarily occupy, that's a matrimonial home. You don't need a document saying that. If you have a cottage that you ordinarily occupy a few weeks each year, that's a matrimonial home. You can have as many matrimonial homes as you live in. Investment properties don't count. You have to live in it together at some point in the year.

All provinces are in agreement that one spouse should not be able to do anything to dispose of or encumber the property without the consent of the other spouse. So, your spouse should not be able to put a mortgage on the property without you knowing. Nor should he be able to sell your home out from under you. I say shouldn't because there are always stories that belie the *shoulds* of life.

While ownership is one question, possession is yet another. In some provinces—most, in fact—regardless of who actually owns the home, both parties are entitled to possession. So either you or your ex can apply to the court to give you sole possession of the matrimonial home regardless of whose name appears on the deed. This exclusive possession can be a valuable right, particularly in cases where there is family violence.

If a matrimonial home at the date of separation was the same home lived in at the date of marriage—he owned the house, you moved in when you got married, or you owned a house, sold it, and used the proceeds to buy a new home into which you both moved when you married—then the original home-owner cannot deduct its value prior to the marriage when calculating the NFP. Ouch!

You are going to have to consider the likelihood that your family home may have to be sold to equalize. If this appears to be the case, you'll need to begin looking for an alternative home for you and your kids. It also means "guestimating" how long it will take to sell the home so you have an idea of when you'll need to take possession of the new property, whether you are buying or renting. Check the real estate market in your neighbourhood to see how fast properties are turning, and how close to the value you are likely to get.

It costs a pretty penny to pack up a household and move. Before you negotiate the final settlement, make sure you've included estimates from moving companies so that your settlement covers it. And don't forget to find out how any insurance or tax rebates will be divided.

Determined to keep the house? Many women are. They cite continuity for their children—same schools, same neighbours, same friends. They cite the inability to cope with one more change with everything else going on. They cite the fact that they love the house. Whatever your reason may be, if you want to keep your existing home, you'll have to look into ways to finance the equalization, in essence to buy out the other's share. A new mortgage, a line of credit, and a second mortgage are all options. Keep in mind that the more debt you take on, the harder it's going to be on your cash flow once you find yourself on your own. But if it means that much to you, you'll find a way. If you don't have credit or the financial means yourself, parents and relatives may be willing to help.

If you are planning to buy another home, make sure your credit history is nice and shiny, and shop around to see how much you'll qualify for on your own. In addition to the down payment, you will need enough money to pay legal fees, insurance, property taxes, and various closing costs. So you need to know what price home you can realistically afford before you go shopping. A pre-approved mortgage can help you determine that.

Resist the urge to fight over the stuff in the house. Disputes over furniture and personal property can be expensive. Think about how to fairly evaluate and divide personal property. If you get carried away with the sentimental value of your stuff—letting emotion rule where reason should—you could end up paying your lawyers a lot more money to fight over that rug, dining room furniture, and entertainment system than it would cost to replace them.

Arming Yourself with the Financial Facts

Whether you're leaving the relationship or you're the one that has been left, at some point you have to gather all the information to arm your lawyer with enough to get you your fair share of the family assets. One of the most important documents you'll be asked to complete is the financial statement. This is the document that will be used to determine how property will be divided and support awarded, and so a lot rides on its accurate completion. Trying to avoid listing assets doesn't work, as the lawyers for both sides will compare your and your spouse's statements. If there was ever a time you did not want your credibility to come into question, this is it. So be honest. If you end up in court, you and your financial statements will be cross-examined vigorously.

One section of the financial statement includes a budget with 69 different types of expenditures, to help figure out the family's spending pattern and what that spending pattern will likely be in the future. If you don't know what you're paying for taxes, entertainment, vacations, food, rent, or medical expenses, you won't be able to paint a clear and complete enough picture for the judge. Include everything. Just because you have a drug plan doesn't mean you don't need a drug budget. Think of all the things that aren't covered by the plan: headache, cold and allergy medicine, antibiotic cream and Band-Aids, potions for diarrhea, stomach upset, and nausea. Anything purchased without a prescription is not covered, so everyone needs a drug budget.

Leavees have one up on this because they can begin gathering info before their partners are aware they should be hiding stuff. Leavers often have to scrounge around, dig deeper, and resort to deceit and skullduggery to gather information. It doesn't really matter what you have to do to get the information… just do it!

Typically, women who are being left are far less aware of their family's financial picture than are the men in their lives. And while many a marriage has lots of loot buried deep in the family files, most women who have not been involved in the financial side of things have no idea of where to begin looking.

A false assumption women often make is that the legal system is fair and that it will all come out in the wash. This is simply not true. There are hundreds of stories of women who have been awarded far less than was fair because they did not do their homework.

Taking Control of Your Financial Life

Divorce brings with it new economic freedom. At first overwhelming, particularly if a body has never had to deal with the money before, the greater sense of control is often empowering. According to sociologist Catherine Riessman, "Managing money is both a symbolic and a tangible way to measure freedom and to project a new and positive self."[1] Particularly interesting in Riessman's study are the differences in how men and women view their economic freedom. While men spent more lavishly on themselves—things like hobbies, trips, sports, and even hair replacement (Joe has to look good now that he's back out hunting)—women felt they were acquiring a greater sense of competence in learning how to handle the bills and in earning their own money. And, while women's economic circumstances were significantly affected by the divorce, rather than whining about not having as much as they did, these newly divorced women see themselves as "active agents, taking charge by opening bank accounts, establishing credit, and deciding how to spend what they have."[2]

Jennna's Story

When my husband left, I had no idea what to do about the money. He'd always done it and I was sure he always would. Besides I just don't have the mind for money. I was lousy with it, and it was good to have someone else take over. I did work for a while when we were first married, but once Barry and Natalia were born I stayed home. Jerry left when Barry was just 3 and Natalia was 5. He said he'd fallen in love with someone he met at work. I never suspected. I didn't even know who the woman was.

The next few months were really tough. We didn't have an agreement yet and Jerry was giving me money every week but it just didn't seem to be enough. He kept paying the mortgage and the other household bills. But I kept running out of money so I kept sticking stuff on my Visa. Finally, when I met with a lawyer and we worked out the numbers it became apparent that we were broke. The mortgage was costing a fortune. The kids were both in Montessori and that was costing almost $800 a month. I had over $5,000 on my credit card and we had a personal line of credit for about $25,000. I remembered signing the paperwork for the line of credit, but I had no idea we were so far into it.

We had to sell the house. Jerry didn't object to paying for the kids 100 percent until I got myself a job. It was a very big change for all of us. But it was bound to happen. I'm sorry now that I wasn't more aware of what was going on. I feel like I chased him away because I didn't know how much stress he must have been under.

When I finally landed a job, it turned out to be a pretty good one. Jerry still makes more than me, so we split the cost of the children 60/40. We're living in a much smaller house, but we're just a walk to the local school. Daycare became a lot less expensive when Barry went into Grade One, so I suggested that Jerry and I start putting some money away in an RESP for the kids' university costs. Jerry balked at first. The idea of having extra money in his pocket was appealing. But our separation agreement says he'll cover post-secondary costs, so he finally agreed that if I was willing, he was too.

I know what I'm doing with my money now. It took a divorce and two or three really tough years, but I'm well on my way. I feel finally like I'm in control of my life and it feels really good.

Okay, you're divorced. Or you're almost divorced. You've never handled the money. You have no idea where to start. Baby, this section is for you. Time to grit your teeth, grab a pencil, eraser, calculator, and paper, and start constructing your financial life. Don't forget that financial statement you had to complete and give your lawyer—it has a wealth of information on it. (If, during this exercise, you find you've left stuff off your financial statement, no sweat. You have the option of filing updated statements right up until a settlement is negotiated or ordered by the court.) If you've got a computer, you can use a program such as Quicken to get and stay financially organized.

The first thing is to figure out how much you have and how much you owe. This is your *net worth*, and it gives you a starting point from which to grow financially (see Appendix D). If you're doing a net worth statement prior to your financial settlement, make a note to yourself to update it when your settlement is finalized. Do not avoid doing the net worth statement simply because you're awaiting your settlement. I know one women who's watched her children go from wee ones to teenagers and she still hasn't worked out the money part of her divorce. Don't put your life on hold.

The next step is to make a spending plan (Appendix E). Pessimists like to refer to this as a budget. I don't like that word. "Budgeting" feels like trying to squeeze a size nine foot into a size eight shoe—ouch! A spending plan, on the other hand, is a little more like having your foot measured before you decide which shoes to try on. You can take most of your information from your recently completed financial statement. If it's been six months or more since you did your financial statement, it may be worth doing the calculations again, since a lot can change in six months.

Your Spending Plan

If you've managed to get this far without a spending plan, you'll need one now. And if you're not familiar with how the money flows in and out of the family pocketbook because your spouse has always taken care of it, it's time to get with the program.

What does it cost you to live each month? Go ahead, take a guess. Most people underestimate their expenses because they forget the things that don't occur every month. Did you include your house insurance? How about the cost of your daughter's haircuts, your son's glasses or your makeup? Did your kids go to camp? What about the cat's vet bills, the gifts you buy for your children's friends' birthday parties, the extra trimmings you pick up for Easter, Halloween, Thanksgiving? And what about the two dollars here and five dollars there your kids hit you up to see a movie or to buy Pokémon cards? Doing your cash-flow management in your head is one sure way to forget things—sometimes important things. You've got to write it down. Voilà: a spending plan.

A spending plan is a way of keeping track of the money you get and the money you spend. It gives you a very clear picture of your financial reality. Now, don't relate being proactive about what you're spending with having to give up things you enjoy. A spending plan gives you the freedom to enjoy yourself, because you don't have to worry about how you'll pay the bill when it comes in. You'll know, right from the start, whether you can afford a new coat or not.

If you currently struggle to make it from one paycheque to the next, you may be surprised when you take the time to do a spending plan and realize just how much you spend on impulse purchases: lunches, parking tickets, candy.

A spending plan is made up of two parts: income and expenses. *Income* is the money that comes in. It's your salary or commission, dividend- or interest-income, alimony, child support, pension, disability income, and the like. It is all the money you receive, whether it comes in monthly, quarterly, or in some other timeframe. It does not include money you think you might get. So, if your bonus is not guaranteed, then don't include it in your spending plan. After all, if it doesn't flow in when you expect, and you've already planned to spend it, you'll be up the creek. Better to not include it, and then use it to boost your savings or cover a long-wished-for holiday. *Expenses* are the items for which you have to pay. These represent your monthly costs in after-tax dollars. When you pay amounts annually—insurance, camp fees, tuition—divide these amounts by 12 (or whatever number is applicable) to come up with a monthly amount so you can work these expenses into your plan.

Ready to get to work? First, gather all your bank statements, credit card bills, and whatever other records you have of how you spent your money for the past two years. If you do it for only one year, your figures may be skewed by unusually high or low bills in a particular year. Next, make a category for each bill: heating, telephone, food, clothes, vet bills, gym fees, child care, health, gifts—*everything*. Total each category and divide by 24; that's your monthly average. Now add all the category averages together. This is the amount you spend each month.

Surprised by how much you're spending? Is it more or less than you thought? If you are spending more than you are bringing in, you need to make more or spend less. Start by trimming. Think about how much you want to spend for each category in your plan. Notice that I used the word "want." *You* are in charge of this. *You* say how much you will or will not spend. You can keep right on digging a hole, or you can decide to take control. A spending plan isn't carved in stone. It needs to be able to roll with the punches as unexpected expenses arise, which they will. So include a category for *unusual expenses* in your plan.

Having done all the work to come up with the numbers for your spending plan, now comes the really tough part: the discipline to use it. A spending plan has three columns:

1. *Planned* is the money you expect to spend on each of these areas. For example, you may plan to spend $50 a month on children's clothing.

2. *Actual* will show the amount you had to lay out. Even if you're superb at planning, it's unlikely you'll spend $50 each and every month on your kids' clothes. However, in September, as you ready them for school, you may find you spend considerably more than $50. If you spend $275, this is the figure that would go in the actual column.

3. *Difference* is the difference between what was planned and the actual amount spent. If you've spent more than you planned, the difference is followed by a minus (-) sign to indicate you exceeded your spending plan. If you spent less, use a plus (+) sign to show you're on the positive side.

Going off track in a particular category one month is no reason for panic. It just means you'll have to be a little creative. Look at other categories and see where you can adjust to make up the difference. For example, if you planned to spend $600 a year on clothes, but blew your budget by October, you could either stop buying clothes, or you could steal the money from your holiday category. It's your choice.

Most people who don't want to use a spending plan say one of two things: "I don't have the time" or "I don't want to be a slave to a system." If you don't believe you can find the time to do this for even three months, consider this: a sad statistic shows that Canadians on average spend 10 hours a year taking care of their money and 1000+ hours a year watching TV. You'll have to decide where your priorities lie. If you don't want to be a slave to the system, you don't have to be. This is a habit that comes naturally after a little practice. I redo my spending plan every 10 months or so, and I cross check with it to see how I'm doing every quarter. Establishing any new positive habit takes time and a little effort so, if you've never lived with a spending plan before, you've got to be religious about it until you get the hang of it. If you don't want to, nothing I can say will make a difference. You'll continue to come up short, worry, and find yourself in the red. That's your choice. You're a big girl, you can decide.

Don't forget to include your lawyer's cost. And if you're depending on support, be prepared for lags in income, particularly if your divorce is acrimonious. You had better have an emergency fund.

Your Emergency Fund

There may be interruptions in your income as you go through the divorce, particularly if your husband is ticked off with the amount of spousal or child support granted to you, so have a stash of cash at the ready to fill the gaps. That may mean taking money from a joint account, pulling on a joint line of credit or, in extreme circumstances, taking advances against a supplemental credit card.

Yes, I am advocating getting the money from whatever source available to protect yourself. The road through divorce can be long and bumpy and you may have to lay out a lot of cash along the way. Document where you've taken the money from so you can provide it to your lawyer (and to your ex's lawyer), identifying the fact that you know this will be flushed out in the accounting and final division of assets.

If you're in the house with the kids, you can't risk missing mortgage payments. If an unusual expense arises—the furnace goes or the car dies— you'll need money. Remember, you don't know what you're getting into in your separation or divorce. You'll still have to pay bills and keep food on the table. You can't afford to be left without money while your husband, the lawyers, and the courts try to decide how much it costs for you and your children to live. If you think this is extreme, it only seems so because you haven't yet had to live from week to week without money.

Michelle's Story

When Tony left I was stranded. I had to keep up with the mortgage payments, pay for Diana's daycare, buy food … there were weeks when we both ate cereal for dinner. I asked my parents for help, and they tried, but when the car suddenly died I was completely at the end of my wits. I had already spent the $4,500 in my RRSP. I didn't have enough money to get a new battery. Diana's boots were too small. The house was going on the market and I didn't have money to paint like the real estate agent suggested. I finally went to the bank. I explained everything and the woman there was very nice. I'd been banking there for a while so she knew me from when Tony and I came in to do our RRSPs. She agreed to give me a small loan until the house was sold. Thank heavens it sold fast. I ended up paying off that loan six months later. I'm still banking there. That woman saved my life.

Your Credit Identity

I am constantly astounded at the number of people I meet who are in a bind because they have no credit history and, so, can't borrow money on their own strengths. This is something we associate with older, widowed women, long cared for by loving, controlling spouses who have now left them to their own devices. But that's just part of the story. First off, not having a credit history isn't the domain of slightly out-of-touch women—there are men out there who haven't got a clue because their wives do everything.

And it isn't the exclusive territory of older people—there are young professionals who haven't bothered to establish their own credit identities.

Everyone needs to have the ability to borrow money. That's true whether you are in the new role of single parent without an emergency fund, or a fifty-year-old woman striking out on her own. And the fastest, cheapest and easiest way to establish a credit history is with a credit card.

The first time you borrow, you will likely need to have either a co-signer or sufficient assets to secure the loan. If you've been divorced recently and have assets to secure a loan, that won't be too difficult. If you don't, then you may have to turn to a co-signer to get yourself in the door. Most people overlook credit cards as an option because they don't realize a credit card can be secured.

A secured credit card is the fastest way to get a credit record. With a secured credit card, you put up cash to cover your balance. Lenders often want twice the credit-card limit, so if you want a $500 credit limit, you'll have to ante up $1,000. Once you've established your ability to manage the card—anywhere from six months to a year—you can ask for the security requirement to be dropped and your deposit returned. (Make sure you're being paid interest on your deposit while the credit card company has it in their hot little hands.)

Secured or unsecured, a credit card can be the cheapest way to build your credit file. In the old days, you had to take a loan, which you then repaid to establish yourself. All the while the interest clock was ticking. So you were buying your credit history. With a credit card, you can build a credit record without it costing you a cent. That's because credit cards let you use the issuer's money for a specific period of time interest free. And as long as you repay the outstanding balance in full every month, you can continue to use that credit at no cost. What a deal!

In terms of ease, the hopping credit-card market means issuers are pretty well throwing cards at consumers these days. Just pick one, fill in an application, and see what happens. Of course, as a smart credit shopper, you'll educate yourself before choosing your credit supplier. You'll learn, for example, that

- there are three kinds of credit cards: Travel and entertainment cards (American Express, Diners Club) don't have preset spending limits but must be repaid in full each month. Company or retail store cards (Sears, Shell) are accepted by the issuing company and usually charge the most outrageous rates. Bank cards (Visa, MasterCard) let you "revolve" credit by paying a portion of your balance each month.

- teaser rates—those low interest rates offered as an enticement for you to sign up for the card—last only three to six months. Then the card's higher interest rate kicks in. So if you must carry a balance, pay attention to the terms and the expiry period so you don't get caught paying exorbitantly high interest.

- the type of credit consumer you are should dictate the type of card you have. If you find yourself carrying a balance, search for a new card with the lowest rate and transfer your balance to that new card. If you pay off your balance every month, you might want one of those more expensive cards—who cares, you're not paying interest anyway—that also offers frequent flier miles, cash back, or special insurance options. Just make sure the payoff is worth the price of the annual fee.

Credit cards can be invaluable when it comes to establishing a credit history. Get one, charge everything, pay it off—all off—every month, and in no time flat you'll have a credit history that will earn you preferential rates when next you need to borrow money.

Paula's Story

When I divorced two years ago I discovered that all my credit cards were held jointly with my husband. I used a MasterCard and made all my payments on time. Dick used the Visa and wasn't quite as punctual. Since both cards where held jointly, my credit ended up being affected by Dick's dumb late payments. I didn't even think to write the credit card companies to tell them to take my name off the Visa. When I finally got smart and decided to get a card of my own, no one wanted to give me one. They said because I had less household income and

> my credit history was pretty well destroyed, I was too much of a risk. It was so unfair. I was the one who always paid on time. But because he had all the income, he had no problem.

If you're holding cards on which you are jointly liable with your spouse, call and have those cards cancelled and new cards issued solely in your name. If you don't and your better half decides to run those cards to the max, you'll be equally liable. The fact that you're deep in the throes of a nasty divorce is of no interest to your creditors. They will haunt you—"You owe us money, honey"—regardless of who spent the money. The same holds true after the divorce. If you are signed for debt obligations with your spouse, having him assume those obligations through your separation agreement isn't enough. You must go the next step and have your name removed as one of the obligated.

Karen's Story

After we divorced I thought that was that. He was to go his way, and me mine. And everything was fine for about three years. Then his company started to run into trouble and the next thing I knew he had declared personal bankruptcy. Of course, he didn't tell me. I found out when the first creditor called to try and collect from me. I informed them we were divorced. They didn't care. I had signed the bank loan and they were going to get their money one way or another. It didn't matter that I had a separation agreement that specifically stated that he was responsible for that debt. I was still on the original paperwork at the bank and so they came after me with all their guns. It was a very trying time. I lost just about everything I'd worked for in those three years. There I was back to ground zero. I still can't believe my lawyer never told me to go to the bank with the separation agreement and get my name removed from that loan. I just never thought about it.

If you have a line of credit at the bank on which you are jointly signed with your partner, go and have your signature removed, if you can. If you can't, then write a letter which you hand-deliver to the bank that says, "As of today's date, no cheque can be drawn against this line of credit without both signatures." That way, no one is doing anything without the other's knowledge.

Don't forget to change the PIN number for your bank card.

Investing in Yourself and Your Kids

Now that you're completely dependent on yourself, if you're not taking care of your future, no one is. If you have earned income, you should be contributing to an RRSP. Get on a periodic investment plan. You can start with as little as $25 a month. If you think you can't afford to be investing for your future because your present costs so much, ask yourself this question: If I don't save for my future, what will I live on when my future becomes my present? If you think you have plenty of time to catch up, ask yourself what you did with the last five years of your life and how much you would have today if you had started back then. If you think the government is going to take care of your future, here's a gentle reminder: you thought your husband was going to do that too. You can't depend on anyone but yourself.

Make sure when you negotiate your settlement that you include a provision for the future education of your children. Your separation agreement should specifically state who is responsible for post-secondary education. While the he'll-take-over-after-high-school condition may seem fine, what will you do if he just doesn't have the resources? Or suppose he dies before all your kids have made it through university? Better to establish a systematic savings plan for each child—be it a Registered Educational Savings Plan (RESP) or in-trust account—so that you can be sure the money will be there when it comes time for your kids to head off to the halls of higher learning.

Insuring Your Safety

Tanya's Story

Jack and I were married for seven years. We worked hard and played hard together. We were each other's partners and best friends. The last two years were horrible for us. I got pregnant and very ill. After three months the doctor ordered me into bed. Jack and I barely spoke. I was too sick, he was so busy. After Muriel was born it got worse. I had the baby to look after. She was colicky and I was up all night with her. I was tired and so was Jack. We fought about little things at first, and then bigger things later. Then it just ended. I can't remember which of us broke first, but it doesn't matter, we both knew we were unhappy. Muriel was the best and worst thing that happened to us. We both love her to bits but I can't help feeling she put this huge strain on our marriage.

Last year I was diagnosed with multiple sclerosis. I had just got a new job so my company benefits hadn't even kicked in yet. They weren't that great anyway. I've been off for three months with no money. Jack's been trying to help, but he remarried and his new wife is in school so they're living on one income. She's not really thrilled that he's giving me money. My child support covers most of the mortgage, and my employment insurance benefits make up the difference, along with taking care of the food and utilities. But there is nothing extra. I'm 37 years old and I don't know how I'm going to make it through the rest of my life. If I go into remission again I'll be able to go back to work, but I seem to be getting weaker all the time. Some days I can't even button Muriel's jacket, my fingers on my right hand are so weak.

If you considered your partner to be your disability plan, it's time to get a real disability plan; one that will be with you in any eventuality. In any given year, regardless of your age, there's a one in three chance that you'll become disabled.

If you have a pre-existing medical condition that may preclude you being covered for disability or health insurance, you need to ensure that your settlement in some way offsets your inability to secure your new, smaller family's financial future. Have an insurance specialist review the insurance you will likely need once you're on your own so you can negotiate effectively through your divorce.

Whether you're looking at disability insurance or life insurance, what you are really buying is cash when you need it most. You're buying replacement for the income you would have had if you had not become disabled or had not died. And you're shifting the risk to the insurance company instead of assuming the risk yourself. If you have no form of income-replacement insurance, you're betting that you'll just keep on chugging along till a ripe old age. Wake up! If you're 30 years old, there's a 23 percent likelihood that you'll die before you reach age 65. And there's a 52 percent probability that you'll be disabled for 90 days or more.

Find yourself a qualified insurance advisor before you go shopping for disability insurance. There are so many variables involved in buying disability insurance, you'll need a guide to show you which ones are worth your money and which ones aren't.

Life insurance is just as important as health and disability insurance. If your ex isn't in the picture a whole lot—some husbands do move away and start new lives, as if their previous lives and families never existed— then you must have life insurance to protect your children. And don't bother with the old "I don't believe in insurance" argument. You have a responsibility to provide the guardians of your children with sufficient financial resources to be able to provide for those kids without it being an economic hardship. Love is fine; money helps too.

Whether or not you need to buy life insurance depends on

- how much you currently have in assets
- how much debt you have
- how much your family will need to make ends meet
- whether you're concerned about minimizing the tax impact on your estate

As a quick test, read through the following questions. If you answer no to any, you'll likely need some insurance.

Will your estate have sufficient funds to

- take care of your funeral expenses?
- pay your accounting, legal, and probate fees?
- pay taxes owing at death?
- provide sufficient income to meet your family's day-to-day needs?
- eliminate any debts you have at death?
- provide for other areas of priority, such as the education?

Another good use of life insurance is to protect the stream of child support payments you may be receiving from your ex. Any good lawyer will advise you to write into your separation agreement that your husband take out and pay for an insurance policy that will guarantee your children support until they reach a specific age. While the separation agreement and support order are binding on your ex-spouse's estate, if the estate doesn't have enough to fund the support, that's pretty well that. And, of course, if your ex agrees, you can insure his life, pay the premiums yourself and have a party when he departs this earth.

As for health insurance: if your spouse belongs to a group health plan, your joint dependent children should still be covered under that plan. But you won't be, so make sure you get a medical plan of your own.

You also need to be aware of how your homeowner and auto insurance will be affected by your divorce. Don't go cancelling insurance on the other guy just because you don't want to have his ugly face anywhere near yours over the next few trying months. Keep everyone and everything covered until all the i's are dotted and t's crossed. Otherwise a liability claim or casualty loss could wipe out the assets you have accumulated. This is also the time to begin exploring liability and casualty coverage options for the future.

If you're planning to sell the family home and rent for a while—a breathing space is always a good idea—you'll need tenant's insurance to cover your personal property. It's also a good idea to include in your emergency fund an amount equal to your deductibles so, if disaster strikes, you're covered.

Staying Ahead in the Tax Game

If you plan on receiving support—whether for yourself or your children—then your financial planning for divorce must begin even before you negotiate your separation agreement. That's because there are special rules for how spousal and child support are taxed.

Spousal support is deductible for the payer, and is included in the income of the payee, as long as the recipient is receiving support as directed by a written separation agreement or court order, and those payments are made on a periodic basis. This only applies to people who have been legally married. If you've just cohabited, you'll need a court order to have your paid support deemed deductible by the taxman. Revenue Canada recognizes payments made on a periodic basis one calendar year prior to the year your separation agreement is signed: if you sign a separation agreement in 2001, you can go back as far as January 1, 2000, to claim periodic payments made.

In the year of separation you have a choice between claiming payments made or the spousal credit. If you legally separated in December, it might be worth more to claim the spousal credit than a single month's support payment. Do the math before you make the choice. Also note that the same flexibility applies if you and your spouse decide to make another go of it, and is applicable for the year the reconciliation takes place.

As of May 1, 1997, child support is not included in income of recipient. Nor is it deductible for the payer. For support orders made prior to 1997, payments are deductible by the payer and included in the income of payee.

As a single parent, you can claim the equivalent-to-married credit for one of your children. You can also claim all your child-care costs—everything from occasional babysitting to a nanny—as long as you get a receipt. You don't have to submit those receipts with your return, but you must keep them just in case Revenue Canada asks for verification.

If you have children in university, make sure they file their own returns. Children who do not need to claim all their tuition fees to reduce their federal tax payable to zero can transfer those fees to you.

Your Estate Plan

When you divorce, any benefit to your former spouse under your will is revoked. But that automatic revocation does not apply to places where you may have designated your ex as your beneficiary: RRSPs, insurance, and the like. You have to do that yourself. What are you waiting for?

If your ex has Power of Attorney for your financial or personal care, remember to ditch him. Don't think this applies to you? What about the brokerage account you opened where your husband may have been making most of the calls, and you executed a power of attorney to give him the right to trade on your behalf? It's amazing what we'll sign when we're happily married that can turn against us when we're unhappily divorcing. It doesn't matter how long you've been married or what a nice guy your ex is—if you have signed paperwork that you have not kept copies of, get to work to collecting it all back.

5

Non-Traditional
Families

The concept of family is changing, here in Canada and around the world. It's nice to be able to say that Canada is at the forefront in legislating changes that recognize that families come in all shapes and sizes. It's time we stopped judging each other and recognized that we all have our own path to walk, that we each have a role in helping each other to make it, and that exclusion is unconscionable.

Whenever a relationship ends, the people in that family unit suffer. We need laws that protect all the members of the family, not just those that have until recently been legally included in what was recognized as family. We still have a way to go, but we are making progress. Still, if you're one of those people who have lived in a non-traditional family and your relationship is ending, there are things you need to know about how your circumstances—and the law's response to them—are different.

Common-Law Relationships

Over the past 25 years, the number of common-law unions in Canada has steadily increased. According to the Vanier Institute, more than 20 percent of couples under 40 are living in common-law relationships. And about four of every ten common-law couples are raising children. In fact, between 1990 and 1995 there were as many common-law unions as marriages.[1]

Statistics also show that there's considerably less stability in a common-law family than in a marriage. As many as 70 percent of first common-law relationships end in separation within the first five years. It is as if we are now trying on our partners before we decide to keep them. This instability isn't slowing the trend to common-law unions. It is supposed that half of all Canadian women born between 1971 and 1980 will have a common-law relationship at some point, making it the preferred conjugal state for their first union.[2]

The End of a Common-Law Relationship

If you and your partner have been living together for three years, or if you have a child together, family law recognizes you as a married couple and you have the right to ask for support. However, you must request spousal support within two years of the end of your relationship or you'll lose the right.

Special note: Many laws have their own definition of a common-law relationship. While the general definition is "two people who have cohabited in a conjugal relationships for three years, or are the natural or adoptive parents of a child," the actual timeframe differs based on the law you're looking at. Since people who have cohabited for just one year are considered common-law under the tax codes, they can claim each other as dependents and contribute to RRSPs for each other.

In a common-law relationship, each partner keeps his or her own property, since common-law spouses acquire no property rights other than those that any other two persons living together (such as a brother and sister) might acquire. But the law does give one partner a right to a share in the other partner's property in some circumstances. The courts look at many factors, including the intention of the common-law husband and wife, the length of the relationship, the financial contributions of the parties, and how title is registered. While various types of claims can be made, they are usually based on one partner having made a direct or indirect contribution to the acquisition or preservation of some item that the other person owns. So while your partner may have bought that antique dining-room table and chairs at the auction, the fact that you lovingly and painstakingly refinished them weighs in your favour. Similarly, while your partner may have paid the mortgage all these years, the fact that you managed the upkeep and improvement of the property says something about your interest in the asset. You may also have a right to share your partner's CPP benefits.

The same goes for your debts. You're each responsible for your own, but are both responsible for household debts such as rent. And you're responsible for your partner's tax liabilities, too.

When a common-law relationship ends, both parents continue to have parental and financial responsibility for the child. If you can't decide on custody and access arrangements, the courts will, based on the best interests of the child. The amount of child support awarded will depend on your child's needs and your income.

Same-Sex Relationships

The struggle for gay rights took a historic leap forward on May 20, 1999, when the Supreme Court of Canada—in a decisive 8–1 judgment—declared that gay couples are no different than heterosexual couples in their ability to share loving unions and suffer when those relationships founder.

The exclusion of same-sex partners from the benefits of the spousal support scheme implies that they are judged to be incapable of forming intimate relationships of economic interdependence, without regard to their actual circumstances. Taking these factors into account, it is clear that the human dignity of individuals in same-sex relationships is violated by the definition of "spouse" in s. 29 of the FLA [Family Law Act].

Speaking directly to a case challenging Ontario's Family Law Act, the Supreme Court said that gay couples should have the same rights to support payments as do their common-law peers. They gave Ontario six months to comply, nodded at the other provinces that they should follow, and established a landmark position that was being closely watched around the world.

Shortly after this ruling, two men who had challenged Nova Scotia's definition of spouse were allowed to collect CPP survivor benefits. Within a month, Quebec provided homosexual couples the same rights as common-law pairs. And B.C. had already changed several laws, including a

1996 decision to allow adoption by same-sex couples. The federal government is also planning to amend almost 60 federal statutes to include gays and lesbians, including pension and income-tax laws.

By October 1999, the Ontario government finally granted, albeit grudgingly, same-sex partners the same rights enjoyed by heterosexual couples. The new bill complied with the Supreme Court of Canada decision in May that same-sex common-law couples are entitled to sue each other for alimony, among other things. But the Conservative government failed to grant same-sex couples status as spouses under Ontario law, in effect dealing with the legal aspects without managing to incorporate the spirit of the Supreme Court's ruling. However, no matter how unenthusiastic the government was in embracing the idea that all couples, regardless of sexual orientation, are in fact couples, the change is a move in the right direction.

The Law Commission of Canada, a federal agency that advises Ottawa on law reform, is examining the prospect of extending benefits to all relationships. One option is to create "registered domestic partnerships." Couples who sign up would then be legally recognized. It has been done in Europe, and considered in B.C. and Alberta. But the implementation has varied, with some applying the idea strictly to same-sex relationships, while others have included extending the definition of family even further to include just about everyone you've ever come into contact with.

Interestingly, a survey commissioned by the federal Justice Department and conducted by Angus Reid in 1998 to measure public opinion on same-sex benefits, also suggested that 71 percent of Canadians either strongly or somewhat agreed that benefits should not depend on marriage, but on any relationship of economic dependency in which people live together. So if your Great Aunt Sally has been supporting you since the day of dot, you could sue her for support if she finally becomes sick of being the proverbial feedbag. This is not, I'm sure, what the Supreme Court intended when it ruled in the M. v H. case that a gay couple who shared an intimate spousal relationship had the same rights as any other couple.

Step-Relationships

Denise's Story

Matthew and I were divorced five years ago. When we first married, I was work-ing. Dillon, my three-year-old from my previous marriage, was in daycare, which his dad paid for directly. After I got pregnant with Samantha, Matthew wanted me to stay home. We fought about it for a while, but when I got pregnant with Allison almost immediately, I gave up the fight. Three kids under six were enough to keep me home. So when Matt and I split up I was really surprised at his attitude toward Dillon. He said there was no way he was supporting some other guy's kid, that it was Dillon's dad's responsibility and that he was mine not his. He'd been Dillon's dad for six years and all of a sudden any concern he had, or maybe he pretended to have, suddenly vanished. By this time Dillon's dad was between jobs. He was giving me what he could, but that was just $300 a month, not really enough. I hadn't pushed it because I knew he was doing the best he could and, besides, Matt had taken on the responsibility for Dillon when we married. He even said at one point that he wanted to adopt Dillon, but I couldn't do that to Dillon's dad.

Most step-parents who separate aren't aware of what the law defines as a parent for the purposes of determining child support. The Family Relations Act, which is the law that governs this area, includes step-moth-ers and step-fathers as parents if

- the step-parent has contributed to the support and maintenance of the child for one year or more, including everything from providing a home, contributing to mortgage payments, or sharing in a joint bank account out of which the child's needs are taken care of,

- the step-parent has lived in a conjugal relationship with the child's biological parent for two years or more, and

- the biological parent sues for support within one year of the date when the step-parent last contributed financially to the support of the child.

In the past it was argued that a step-parent would actually have to stand in the place of a biological parent—referred to in legal terms as *in loco parentis*—to be financially liable for the child. But that has been cast aside in an effort to recognize that divorce should affect children as little as possible. In a landmark ruling, Justice Bastarache of the Supreme Court of Canada dismissed the argument that a child might collect support from both a biological and a step-parent, saying all parents have obligations and their contributions should be assessed independently. So a step-parent's liability in no way negates a biological parent's liability for support. The court will actually assess the respective financial obligations of both biological and step-parents.

6

Building Your

Divorce Team

Regardless of how big or small your family assets appear to be, no matter whether or not you have children, no matter how friendly your divorce, you need to have your own team of people to help you through your divorce. Your team may be big or small, depending on how complicated are your finances and how acrimonious is your divorce. For most people, a mediator to help work things out, a lawyer to make it all legal, and an advisor to help establish financial priorities is a good team. For many others, appraisers, real estate agents, accountants, actuaries, estate specialists—they all make up the team.

Your Lawyer

The most influential player on your team will likely be your lawyer. While there are numerous joke books written about lawyers, their ethics and their practices, there are still some trustworthy people out there, and it's your job to find yourself one. One way to locate a lawyer is to contact your provincial law society and ask if they have an accreditation system for family lawyers. Then you can choose two or three in your community for interviews. A better way is to ask your friends who they have used, and what they did or did not like about them, and then do some one-on-one interviewing.

When I was divorcing my second husband, I called a friend who was also a family lawyer and asked her for a reference. She asked me who my ex would be going to. I knew that he had used a particularly high-profile family lawyer in the past, and would likely call on that same lawyer again. When I gave her the name of that lawyer, she immediately responded with, "So you'll have to go to Stephen Grant." You see, it is as much a matter of the lawyers' impact on each other as the impact on your spouse. After all, if you have a wimpy little generalist who doesn't know the game and doesn't have a reputation for playing hardball, you're likely going to end up with less than you would have if you'd hired your own gun. If you think the law is fair, you're wrong. It's all about posturing. It's a political game. And the guy with the best lawyer wins. If you want the game to be fair, you've got to choose a lawyer as good as, or better than, the one your husband bought himself.

Here are some pointers to keep in mind:

- The lawyer you choose should be a family law specialist. You know the old saying, and wouldn't go to a podiatrist to have a baby. Well, it applies to lawyers too. Family law is a very, very specialized area, so you need someone who does it every day, day in and day out, if you expect him to be any good at it. Of course, that doesn't mean that all family lawyers are a) good at their job or b) good for you. Which brings us to...

- The lawyer you choose should come through a referral from a friend, co-worker, friend of a co-worker...whatever. She shouldn't just come from the yellow pages. With a reference, you're already half-way home. You should know at least one person who's happy with the job she's done, and who didn't come from her reference list. Ahhh, now comes the rest of the equation...

- The lawyer you choose should be good for you from a personality point of view. He doesn't have to be just like you—that might not be so good for you. But you should feel comfortable with this person. You should have a sense that you respect his knowledge and opinion, and he should respect yours.

- You don't want a lawyer who is a one-dimensional thinker. You know the type—she booms, "I don't believe in mediation" or "Joint custody, bah!" Instead, look for a lawyer who can think outside the box, can be creative in coming up with alternatives, and uses the services of other specialists—mediators for example—to get the best possible results for you.

- You don't want a head-honcho lawyer who passes you off to an underling. If you hire a lawyer, unless you agree to work with other members of the team such as a law clerk or junior lawyer—and some people do to mitigate the costs of the divorce—you should expect your meetings, conversations, and negotiations to include the lawyer you hired.

- Don't use a lawyer your husband has used in your past life together, or who is associated with your spouse's family. If your divorce turns into a war, you need to know that your lawyer's alliances lie with you and you alone.

- Resist the urge to use the same lawyer as your husband. It doesn't matter how much money you think you'll save, it's a dumb thing to do. There's no way for a lawyer to provide objective advice to two people with opposing interests. If you have to watch pennies, there are smarter ways to reduce the cost of your divorce.

- Whatever you do, don't use your lawyer as your emotional outlet. If you have to arm yourself with a box of tissue every time you step into his office, you're wasting his time and you're paying way more than you need to. Consider your relationship with your lawyer to be strictly business. Don't bitch, whine, cry, complain, plot revenge, or seek consolation. His job is to get you the best possible settlement, help you negotiate the custody arrangement that's best for your children, and get you divorced so you can get on with your life. Need a shoulder to cry on? Call your mother. If she's tired of listening, get yourself into counselling.

Ways to Prepare for Your Lawyer

I remember when I arrived for my first meeting with my divorce lawyer, Stephen Grant. A big, burly guy with a tough reputation and a soft heart, he asked me, "Date of separation?"

I replied, "Today."

"No," he said, "the date you separated from your husband."

"Today," I reiterated.

"But you made this appointment two weeks ago," he responded a little puzzled.

"I plan ahead," I said, as I proceeded to hand him everything I thought he would need to set me free: my marriage certificate, my will, powers of attorney, and myriad other pieces of paper that were the records of my life with my soon-to-be-ex-husband.

One of the best ways to get yourself ready for your trip to the lawyer is to write your story down. Start at the beginning—when you were married, where—and proceed through your life, focussing on the important things. Remember, your lawyer will charge you for reading your tomb, so don't give her your version of *War and Peace*. Things you should include? Your courtship story, when you started living together, how you lived, and details of any counselling you took. Also include your financial history: Who supported whom? What did you do before you were married? Did you work while married? If you stopped work, why? Then comes the family stuff: when the kids were born, what changed with each birth, how you both parent, how you feel about custody and access, including what you would consider perfect and what you would consider unacceptable. Finally, we come to your impressions about what has happened and what you would like—everything from what you think happened to your marriage to what you want for your children and yourself after the divorce. Try to stick to the facts as much as possible. Venting your anger is fine, but you shouldn't be paying lawyer's fees while doing it.

Once you've completed your "history of my relationship as told to myself," wind up by attaching all the important documents you can lay

your hands on. Not sure what you need? Here's a list of the most important stuff your lawyer will need:

- your full legal name, your address (work and home), your telephone
  number, and any other means of contact (cellular, fax, e-mail, etc.);
  include all addresses you've lived at in the past two years

- your date and place of birth, date and place of marriage, and date of
  separation

- the details of all previous marriages, including the surname of your ex-
  spouse, and a copy of your *decree absolute* if it's available

- if you are not a citizen of Canada by birth, you should include the date
  you came to Canada, and the length of residence by province

- if you have children, include their names, their dates of birth, and the
  school(s) and grades they attend

- your spouse's information, including name, date and country of birth,
  residency, address and contact numbers, and the name of your spouse's
  lawyer, if you know it

- financial details for both you and your STBE: level of education,
  employment history, net worth prior to marriage, net worth at separation, contributions made to the family

The final thing you'll need before you show up at the lawyer's office is
moolah. It is the exchange of money that establishes your client-lawyer relationship, so don't think your lawyer's a money-grubbing, insensitive lout
when he asks for a retainer. He'll have plenty of time to prove whether he's
a nice guy or not. For now, just ante up.

Managing the Relationship with Your Lawyer

While we're on the subject of money, this would be a good time to find out
what this divorce is likely to cost. Find out what your lawyer's hourly rate is
at the office and in court—these are often different. Ask how the law clerk's
time is billed. And remember, everything—every telephone call, every
message left, every piece of investigative work, every letter, *everything*—costs

money. Your lawyer's time is the commodity you're paying for, so make sure you're getting something useful for your money. Don't be manipulated. And don't be so overwhelmed by what you perceive as your lawyer's authority that you allow him or her to blow you hither and yon, racking up legal bills and leaving the loves of your life strewn about like so many autumn leaves.

Phyllis's Story

You know, you think when you go to a lawyer to get a divorce that she would have your best interests at heart. But I always felt it was more about the money than about me. She'd call me up and ask how I was doing and after I had vented for a half an hour, I'd feel much better. That is until I got the bill for the telephone call. It got to the point where I'd say, "Don't ask me how I am, because I know it's going to cost me money." Sometimes it even felt as if she was inciting me to riot. She claimed to leave messages for me at home that I never got. She inferred that perhaps "someone"—that would be my ex of course—was erasing her messages. She'd ask for the same details over and over, and each time I'd pay for the privilege of repeating myself. She'd even show up at court and do things I wasn't prepared for. At one point I remember telling her explicitly that I didn't want my son away more than two weeks at a time, but she blithely walked into court and offered my ex three weeks in the summer. Hello. It was like she wasn't even there when we had the conversation. She told me she'd done me a favour. Why did I feel like I'd just been screwed? I tried to fire her a couple of times, but I was so deep into the divorce that I thought it would cost me a small fortune to bring a new lawyer up to speed. It was tough going. Eventually I bit the bullet and got myself a less well-known expert, one who was a little more focussed on me and my son.

Verify your lawyer's billing procedures. The last thing you need is to go merrily along, fighting your ex-spouse, only to find a $50,000 bill at the end of it all. You probably are best off seeing a bill every month to have a good appreciation of what your divorce is costing you. If you're counting on a settlement to pay your lawyer, discuss it and make a plan for repayment that works for you both. Find out what the interest rate will be on the outstanding balance.

The outcome of your divorce will affect the rest of your life, so you should always be aware of where you stand—the pros and cons—when it comes to making any decision. No lawyer can guarantee you results. Any who say they can are bluffing, and you should immediately seek a second opinion. However, your lawyer can, within his experience and the boundaries of the law, explain the range of possible outcomes for your case. Your lawyer will also be able to explain the strong and weak pointsof your case, the worst that you can anticipate, and how long it'll all take based on whether a settlement is reached or you end up in court. All the way along, you need to check on costs.

While you may not be particularly open to hearing this, at some point your lawyer may tell you that some of your goals are unrealistic. It you don't believe that, there's nothing wrong with getting a second opinion. A consultation with a second lawyer will help to put the first lawyer's opinion in perspective for you. If you're still not hearing what you want, the problem may be that you do, in fact, have unrealistic expectations and that it's time to get in touch with reality. It makes little sense, emotionally or economically, to go fighting for lost causes. The smartest clients are those who weigh the likelihood of achieving their most important goals against the time and money involved. It's up to you to decide which battles are worth the expense and effort, and which ones you will have to bite your tongue and walk away from. Having said that, you should never waive important rights just because you want the whole bloody thing to be done with. You, and perhaps your children, will have to live with the decisions you make today a long time into the future.

Ten (or so) Questions to Ask your Lawyer

1. Do you specialize in divorces, or are divorces just a part of your practice? How many divorces like mine did you handle in the past year? How long have you been doing divorce work? How have you handled divorces like mine before?

2. What can you do to help me understand the financial implications of the decisions I will have to make?

3. Will anyone else in your office be working on my case? Can I meet them? (Since many divorce lawyers are hard to catch at the office—they're always in court—you need to feel comfortable with the lawyer's assistant. Do you feel he or she is competent? Easy to talk to?)

4. How will you charge me? What is your hourly rate? Do you charge for the time I spend with other lawyers, paralegals, and/or secretaries? If so, at what rate? What expenses do you expect will be involved and how will you charge me for them? Do you charge for faxes, copies, and long-distance telephone calls? How much? (Some lawyers consider these services an additional profit opportunity.)

5. What do you think this divorce will end up costing me in total? Are there things I can do to help keep the costs down?

6. Do you advocate mediation? What style of mediation do you prefer? In how many cases have you represented a client who was mediating his or her divorce? What mediators would you recommend? If my spouse and I mediate, will I have to pay you to be there the whole time, or can I use you simply as an coach on an as-needed basis?

7. If I decide at any point I'd like to take control and negotiate directly with my spouse or with my spouse's lawyer to save money, will you let me do that, using you as a coach? Or will you insist that all communications flow through you?

8. Based on what you know about my case, what do you think the outcome will be? What facts would make the ruling more in my favour? If my spouse were sitting here with you asking the same questions, how would you answer my spouse?

9. Does your office use the latest technology? (A computer on your lawyer's desk—turned on—may mean your lawyer has to spend less time and less of your money to produce the documents needed for your case.)

10. Have you had any clients or former clients file grievances against you with the bar association? If so, please tell me about them.

As you visit with each lawyer you meet with to interview, trust your judgement. Ask yourself, Do I like this person? Does he seem willing to take the time to listen to what's going on in my life and what I want to accomplish? To explain the options available to me? Does she seem rushed? Does he take phone calls during our meeting? Does she seem distracted or disorganized? Does he smile? Does she appear genuine?

You Got Yourself a Lousy Lawyer, Now What?

Many people allege that some family-law lawyers make a practice of escalating the fight between divorcing people. These practices include encouraging clients to make false claims of abuse, and encouraging women to invoke violence as a way to ensure an advantage in parenting and property disputes.

Donna's Story

I told the lawyer I didn't know what my rights were, that I wanted to end my marriage. I wanted to know, if I left the house, would I lose my entitlement to the property. I was stunned by his answer. He told me to have a huge fight with my husband and get him to strike me. In our 22 years together, he had never struck me. It wasn't right. But he insisted that if I made him hit me, I could keep the house and he'd have to give me spousal support.

I've heard this story, not once, but twice, directly from the women who were involved. The second time I heard it, the details were almost identical, except for the length of time the woman was married. This is a perfect example of how a simple divorce can be turned into a nightmare.

There are also lawyers who take advantage of an emotionally vulnerable client. They suggest unnecessary and costly procedures in the name of advancing their case. If you think you have a lawyer who is working for anyone's best interest but yours, it's time to get a new lawyer. Ditto if your lawyer doesn't return your telephone calls for weeks, doesn't tell you what's going on with your case, or doesn't report (in a meeting or a letter) to you on the status of your case. And if you get bills you don't agree with, make sure you detail your areas of concern in writing. If it comes down to the fact that you want to get rid of your lawyer, you can do so at any time. (Your lawyer isn't allowed to fire you, but a lack of attention to your case will be his version of "Go away!") You'll have to pay off your bill. And you'll likely also have to sit through an exit interview, in which your lawyer tries to determine what went wrong. If you're ticked off enough to want to leave, your lawyer has the right to know why, so don't wuss out; ante up with your criticisms.

Your Mediator

If you think your divorce can only be resolved through an all-out battle, you're making one of two mistakes: you're buying into the myth that divorce has a winner and a loser; or you think that divorce is fair, that it'll all come out in the wash, and that the courts will do what's best for you and your child.

Let's take care of the first myth: There's no such thing as a winner in divorce. You'll both be losers. Now it's just a matter of whether or not you want your kids to be losers, too. As for the fairness of the Canadian family court system—you're in for a mighty big surprise. The system is not fair. It is over-burdened, abused, and sadly lacking in good judgement.

The alternative to divorce war is to accept responsibility for the job of making your kids' lives work. That means cooperation. And that usually means mediation. Mediation provides a confidential, non-adversarial process through which divorcing spouses can negotiate their own settlement with the aid of an impartial third party.

Non-adversarial does not mean there is no conflict. The end of any significant relationship involves such intense emotional turmoil that it is difficult for two individuals to resolve issues fairly without professional assistance. But a commitment to mediation does mean the couple is committed to working together to come to a fair and equitable agreement.

This beats the pants off the traditionally adversarial legal system, where you are pitted against your STBE, and you each try to squeeze, bully, and coerce the best possible deal for yourself through your mouthpieces (your lawyers). In a legal tug-of-war, your children may be pulled into the muddy puddle—and those emotional stains just don't come out. Top that with the fact that your family assets can be significantly diminished as the fight drags on.

Since you and your STBE must continue to be parents together even as you separate, creating a cooperative process through mediation makes good sense. By choosing mediation, the parties talk to each other, rather than through their lawyers, resolving conflicts in less time and at less cost. Mediation gives you and your spouse a way to settle the natural and inevitable conflict between you in a way that helps you to work together as parents after your divorce. Mediation also encourages parents to focus on their children's best interests and to maintain a relationship with their children while designing a parenting plan. In essence, the mediator works for neither you nor your spouse. Instead, the mediator's client is the family. No one person's interest is more important than the other's. It is, instead, the needs of the family that take priority.

A mediator's number-one priority should be to help both you and your ex focus on your children's best interests. Through the development of a parenting plan, you'll retain full control over all decisions, while the mediator will help you explore the alternatives and establish the game rules for dealing with specific issues in the future—anything from whether Jenny should be allowed to go to co-ed all-night sleep-overs, to who will pick up the tab for braces. The mediator helps you focus your energy on the new life you'll be building, not on fighting under the old rules. And since mediated settlements and arrangements reflect a couple's agreement to take ownership of their relationship as parents and ex-spouses, mediation brings a higher level of long-term success.

Of course, not everyone enters mediation with the ability to put the divorce in a nice tidy place and deal maturely and without negative emotion. Truth tell, mediation is often most effective for raging couples. While it won't take the hiss and spit out of a thoroughly nasty divorce, mediators are trained to deal with volatile situations. They will focus on the same issues that would be examined by the court: spousal support, asset distribution, child custody, property settlement, and parenting plans. The difference is that, with a mediator, it is you and your STBE who decide on what is fair.

Hilda's Story

By the time my daughter, Susie, suggested mediation, we had already divided everything up. Why did we need a mediator? We agreed on just about everything. We had no young children; Mark was in his third year of university. The other two kids were married. George made up a list of all our assets and debts. I honestly thought that his pension automatically belonged to him, not realizing that the law considers it a marital asset. He said we'd split the house, that the car was his—which was fine since I don't drive anyway—and that he would give me half of the investments we had. I thought that was fair. I didn't really want much. I just wanted out. But my Susie said she thought I was underestimating my share. So I went to a mediator. When all was said and done, I ended up with almost $200,000 more than I would have if I'd just signed the agreement. Susie was really mad at George for a long time. "You're the one that wanted out," George seethed at me during the mediation. "Why should I have to give you all this money just so you can do your own thing?" I didn't think he was going to budge, but eventually after the mediator suggested he speak to his lawyer, he signed.

Don't make the mistake of thinking that going through mediation eliminates your need for a lawyer. Most mediators recommend that each client consult with a lawyer at some point during the mediation and certainly, before signing the divorce agreement. During the mediation, a lawyer can provide ongoing advice in complicated legal situations. Obviously, the lawyer's attitude toward mediation is critical: the lawyer should be supportive of mediation as well as experienced in divorce work.

And since one of the strengths of mediation is the control participants have over the process, both people must take responsibility for the actions that result. When you give your decision-making power to someone else, it may feel good for the moment, but in the long run, people who do not take part in their own financial and personal decisions often live to regret it. Mediation provides a method to make your own decisions.

Choosing a Mediator

Just as you wouldn't choose a lawyer without first doing some shopping, so too should you shop around for your mediator. Start with references from friends and family. Failing that, make a list of four or five mediators in your area. Talk to them to see which one feels right for you. While you're at it, familiarize yourself with the process, the issues you'll need to discuss, and the costs associated with mediation.

Since anyone can hang up a shingle and claim to be a mediator, one of your first questions should focus on the mediator's training. Find out how long she has been practising. How many divorce cases has he mediated? Is she viewed as an authority? If he's written any articles, served on association boards, trained others or made any speeches on the subject of mediation, he probably knows what he's talking about.

Perhaps the most important issue will be the mediator's style. Some are highly directive, offering evaluation of the likelihood a judge will sign off on one or another option in court, and giving you concrete proposals for resolution of conflicts. Others opt for a more facilitative approach, empowering the couple over and over again to make their own choices through deft questioning and discussion. Neither is right or wrong in theory, but one or the other may be more right for you and your STBE. As you're shopping around, ask mediators to discuss their approaches.

Some mediators offer a free consultation, a great way to get to know the mediator and become familiar with the process. Not everyone does, so ask. Some mediators give the consultation free if the couple continues with the process, and charge a minimal fee if they don't.

Find out your prospective mediator's point of view on the involvement of a lawyer. Good mediators recommend that independent legal counsel reviews the agreement before it is signed.

Unfortunately every profession has its share of charlatans. Mediation is a relatively new profession, and mediators are popping up from all quarters. It's hard to consider switching if, half-way into the process, you believe your mediator isn't the best person for the job—particularly if your spouse doesn't feel the need to switch. But if you get into any of the following situations, switch you must:

• your mediator makes decisions for you

• your mediator takes the side of one person against the other

• your find your mediator is not knowledgeable about divorce laws, taxes, pension rulings, and all other issues of your agreement. The mediator does not need to know everything concerning each area (no one professional is an expert in every area), but should know when such information is necessary and how to get it.

• your mediator has a bias that effects all decisions

• your mediator makes a financial contingency fee arrangement with you. This means that the cost of the mediation depends on the settlement itself; for example, 5 percent of the settlement. Mediation fees should be based on an hourly rate and not contingency arrangements.

Getting Ready to Mediate

Just as you have to gather information to arm your lawyer with the facts of your marriage and life with your STBE, so too should you do some assembling for mediation. Much of the information is the same: a complete disclosure of assets and liabilities, for example. Since you and your spouse will be doing the asset valuation and negotiation yourselves (with the help of the mediator), you'll need to put realistic values on your assets. If you plan to sell your house, for example, one of the things you'll need to agree on is the fair market value. You'll also need to agree on who will pay for what to make the house ready for sale.

Drawbacks of Mediation

If you and your spouse are on relatively friendly terms, and just need to iron out an issue or four, a mediator will be able to get you through relatively inexpensively. However, there are circumstances when mediation is not the appropriate route to take. If you do not have full access to your STBE's financial records, or you think he is holding out on you, you should probably stick with the more traditional adversarial approach. Why? Well, mediation precludes the use of the more formal discovery process through which your lawyer grills your STBE about his finances. I've been in discovery a couple of times and it's quite intimidating and very effective. As well, you should never use a mediator in cases of domestic violence.

The Judge

Most people go to court with one idea—they believe the judge will decide in their favour. Rarely have I met anyone wanting to go to court who assumes they are destined to lose. In some ways, it is a tribute to each person's ability to convince themselves that "I will win once the judge hears what happened." Unfortunately, this naive view of the judge as a kind fatherly protector may be shattered in court. You rarely get a chance to tell your entire story in court and when you do get the opportunity to speak, the parts you think are essential often are not allowed into evidence. The court decision will most likely hinge on technical aspects that seem absurd to someone not versed in the law.

The actual goals of the judge, in fact, may differ radically from yours. Many divorce-court judges share the sentiment of one judge who says, "If I see each of them walking out of court with their head down and looking sad, then I figure I made a pretty good decision." Since there is so much to lose, the court tries to see that neither side loses an unreasonable amount.

The reality of a divorce-court trial is that most people walk out of the courtroom feeling as if they have just been run over by a truck. Even the apparent winner rarely feels good. What looks like winning on the outside often doesn't feel good, either because the spouse feels entitled to much more than what the court awarded, or because he or she feels guilty. The winner may also find his or her enthusiasm dampened by the warning they hear from their lawyer to prepare for the next round, when their STBE will surely appeal the judge's decision. An appeal means another trial, more money, and, of course, the emotional trauma that seems to have no end.

There is another courtroom myth that dies hard: that legal fees are paid for by the party who loses. In most divorce courts, this is simply not true. Whether you win or lose, you will most likely be picking up your lawyer's tab.

Your Financial Advisors

Once you get your share of the family assets, you'll need to take some steps to put that money to work for you. Leaving it in your bank account is too big a spending temptation. Sure, you can set aside a portion to get you back into the game, in terms of furniture that must be replaced or bills that need to be paid off. But the majority of your financial settlement should be invested for the future.

If you've never been the investor in your family you may be confused by the complex array of options available out there in the world of investing. Your first step should be to get yourself a financial guide who can help explain the avenues open to you, and help you avoid making any wrong turns. This person must be a person you can trust. Before you write out the cheque, make sure you're willing to put your financial future in this person's hands.

I take that back. You should never put your financial future in anyone else's hands. That's a sure way to get thoroughly lost. Rather, you should be able to establish a relationship with your advisor that makes it easy for you to ask questions and get the answers you need.

If a portion of your day-to-day cash flow will come from the income you earn on your investments, it'll be of paramount importance that your capital be kept safe and that you generate a decent return after tax. What you won't need are high risks, big fees or commissions—or, on the other hand, the total security and incumbent inflation risk of the tried and true investments. It's a fine balance, no question. But there are good, experienced, thoughtful advisors out there who can help.

Get everything in writing before you decide where to put your money. Whether you're dealing with an insurance salesman, a broker, or a financial planner, make sure the proposed strategy, and the products suggested to implement the strategy, are in writing and easy to understand. At least then, if the strategy isn't followed, you'll have something to work with when you find yourself in arbitration.

You should understand any product you're buying before you buy. And you should understand the rules and restrictions attached if you need to get at your money in an emergency. Always check out the financial stability of the company you're investing with. There have been several accounts of disreputable financial dealings at both the corporate and the advisor level. And remember the golden rule of investing: If it sounds too good to be true, it probably is.

Sorry to say, a designation as a financial planner holds little assurance for a new client. Industry designations are confusing and overlapping and almost anyone can use the title Financial Planner. And since money has become the hot commodity, there are hundreds of advisors with little or no experience.

Be sure to get bank references, client references, and references from professionals, such as lawyers and accountants, who have used the advisor. Ask where the advisor invests money, and why, and find out how the investments are doing. If the prospective advisor won't answer you or hedges, look elsewhere.

Stay away from people who waffle on how they are compensated. Some advisors earn most of their income from commissions on products they suggest to you. Fee-only planners may be more objective than those charging commissions, but their up-front charges may be more. Be sure to find out how many times per year the fee will be charged. Others charge a combination of fees and commissions.

Never give your power of attorney or discretion over your assets to a financial advisor. If you don't understand how a product works, don't buy. If the advisor can't explain it to your satisfaction, find another advisor.

Don't be forced into anything. Don't be intimidated. Get it in writing. Know with whom you are dealing and the strategy that suits you before you deal.

7

Flying
Solo

According to Statistics Canada's 1996 census, the profile of Canadian families continues to evolve. In 1996, common-law and lone-parent families made up 26 percent of all families in Canada, compared to 20 percent a decade earlier. From a historical perspective, the increase in lone-parent families has been particularly dramatic. Between 1981 and 1994, the number of lone-parent families grew by 60 percent. By 1994, 16 percent of children lived in lone-parent families. According to the Vanier Institute, more than four of every five lone-parent families are headed by a single mother. Nationally, almost a third of lone mothers are divorced, a quarter are separated, one in five has never been married, and close to a quarter are widows.

You would think that, with the growth in single-parent families, we would have already come to terms with the myths and issues surrounding single parenthood so that we could get on with the business of living. Not so. Remember the huge fuss Dan Quayle made when Murphy Brown decided to become a single mom; it was the destruction of the family as we knew it. It was a sitcom for goodness sake. And it wasn't creating single parenthood as a model, it was reflecting the reality of what millions of North Americans are experiencing. A vocal group in the U.S. likes to blame violence and other social problems on the disintegration of the nuclear family, but if you buy into these myths, you'll find your job of parenting a whole lot less rewarding than it should be.

Remember why you had these babies. Remember the feeling of their little fingers wrapped around yours, the touch of their soft spots under your chin, the smell of them. Are they any less your family now that you and your ex have split? And is the new life on which you're about to embark really all that different from that of millions of other North Americans? After all, the nuclear family—mom, dad, boy, girl, dog, and canary—is far less the norm since divorce and remarriage have become less of an aberration. Your binuclear family may seem new conceptually, but you're in the majority.

So your home isn't broken. It may have been but, when you divorced, you took the first step to fixing it. And now you're on your way. It may not always be the smoothest of roads—no one's life is, really, it's just that some people are better pretenders than others—but it's your road, and you can make of it what you will.

Now that you're flying solo, one of the smartest things you can do is accept that fact that life is unpredictable for everyone. So on those days when the snow is drifting half-way up the door, the car is frozen locked and your child needs to be rushed to the doctor with an ear infection, it's not your divorce that's to blame, it's just life. And if you get laid off from your job, and wonder how in hell you're going to find another job and keep a roof over your head, and meet your children's expectations, it's not your divorce to blame, it's just life.

Since life can be so unpredictable, a wise single mom also knows just how important planning for the future can be. Since you may be solely reliant on yourself, you've got to put everything in place, so that if something does go awry it doesn't gum up your whole family's works. It means being informed so you also feel in charge. And it means keeping your sense of humour.

Study after study has proven the power of laughter as a healing aid. Researchers say that smiling actually creates physiological changes that provide a sense of well-being. So, when your brain is happy, you are too. And since humour can also be a great parenting tool, laugh with your children a little each day.

Single motherhood brings stereotyped images of a be-robed, unbrushed, scattered, and often forgetful mother who feeds her children fast food and constantly glows blue from the television set. Not exactly dignified, and nowhere near reality. Women who have struggled to raise children or grand-children, bringing home the bacon and frying it up in the pan, know that they are the matriarchs of their families. Matriarch—such a regal word. So stop thinking of yourself as a dishevelled single-mother and think elegant and strong matriarch instead.

Being self-assured is a valuable trait for anyone, but it's invaluable for a single mom. The weight of having to make all the decisions without the input of another adult can sometimes feel intimidating. You need to feel in control. This doesn't come automatically. You need to work at it, and you need to take care of yourself so that ill-health, exhaustion, and loneliness don't sap your precious life energy. Just getting through each day doesn't build confidence or self-esteem. You need to march, waltz, glide through your days. You won't succeed if you try to do it alone. But with your chil-dren on your side, with your friends in the wings, and your support groups just a phone call away, you'll be fine.

Be brave. Courage and confidence go hand in hand. When you feel confident in your decisions, it's pretty easy to muster up courage to explore your new life.

You Can't Do It Alone!

Okay, Supermom, let's get something clear right from the start. You have a new life. You have many more responsibilities. You can't do it alone. You will break if you try, and then what good will you be to yourself or your chil-dren? You need help, and you must be willing to both ask for it and accept it when it's offered.

Your greatest allies should be your children. It may not always appear that this is the case, as your children gloomily or defiantly slump in a chair and whine, "Oh, Mom." But you are a team. And it's your job as team leader to get your team focussed on the projects at hand.

There's no question that, with all the new demands you may be facing, you'll have less time to devote to the household chores. Time to divvy them up. Don't worry, you're not robbing your kids of their childhood. When kids fulfill responsibilities, they gain self-respect and learn competence. When children learn that you depend on them for certain jobs, they feel good about their contribution to the family. While it's always easier if you start when your kids are young, it's never too late. Explain that the responsibilities of running the home have to be shared. Chores aren't a punishment; they're a part of family life.

Let your children be involved in decision making. It's always easier to do tasks you like than ones you don't. So make a list of all the things that have to be done. Everyone's first choice is something they like to do, and the rest get divvied up evenly. Chores shouldn't relate simply to self-maintenance. Children need to see that the whole family counts on them. If they don't follow through, as they should, don't dive-bomb them. Express your disappointment or frustration calmly and ask them to fix the problem. Eventually, they'll get the feeling that their efforts are important to the overall functioning of your family.

Variety is the spice of life, so rotate the jobs your kids do. It'll broaden their skills and eliminate the boredom. Once you assign the job, don't harp on the fact that the job wasn't done right. Rarely will a child do any chore as well as you would, but if you complain you'll take all the satisfaction out of it. Be patient, demonstrate how you like it done, and praise their efforts enthusiastically.

If children simply won't do their chores, don't threaten, scream, or resort to guilt-tripping. Simply point out that if you have to do their chores, there will be other things you may not have time for, such as making their lunches, driving them to the hockey game, or making the costumes for the school play. Don't let this sound like retribution. This is a case of there being only 24 hours in a day. You shouldn't be expected to do it all. Make it clear that whatever time you have to spend out of your day doing their chores will reduce the amount of time you have to do other things with them. A couple of nudges and they'll get the message.

Chores shouldn't take over your life. Having fun is just as important as living in a clean and orderly environment, so pace yourself. Choose two or three rooms each week for deep cleaning, with a view to having the whole place done each month. Everything else gets a spit and polish that week. If you watch the boob tube in the evenings, use the commercial breaks to hold a race in which you all put away the stuff that's out of place

You could also try an incentive chart. List your children's names and chores, and for each completion they get a sticker. A certain number of stickers earns something they like. Make sure the reward is commensurate with the work involved.

Ten Tips for Single Moms

1. Ask for help when you need it. Family and friends want to help but may be unaware you need assistance. Whether it's borrowing money to pay the heating bill or shuttling the kids to and from hockey, just let people know what you need.

2. Always have a back-up plan in case Daddy doesn't show up as planned. Since your kids will be ready to go anyway, load them up in the car and go to a movie, a friend's house or other fun place. This will help offset their disappointment.

3. Establish a good relationship with your child's teacher. You'll have a better idea of what's going on in the classroom, and if problems arise, it'll be easier to find a solution together. Take the time to explain about your home life.

4. Forming a single-parent support group gives you and your children the opportunity to make friends with other families in similar situations. And you and other parents may be able to trade with each other to make all your lives a little easier. For example, you can swap your cooking, babysitting, or bookkeeping skills for someone else's home-maintenance, car-repair, or sewing skills.

5. Children learn from example. What did they learn from you today?

6. Keep your ex-husband informed as much as possible about the children's school and other activities. Regularly send copies of report cards and pictures. Being well informed might make him more receptive to contributing (in terms of time and/or money) to the kids.

7. Make time for family activities at least once a week. Declare one night a week family night. This will help reinforce your family unit. Let each family member have a turn deciding what activity to do for his or her night. Examples: rent/go to a movie, bake cookies, play miniature golf, go to an arcade, visit a museum, ride bicycles.

8. Do NOT use your children as sounding boards or messengers. Do not dump on your kids about your financial woes or their pathetic excuse for a father. Your kids have enough going on in their lives. They don't need your garbage too.

9. Use lists to keep yourself and your kids organized.

10. Establish routines. Habit is a single mom's best friend. Mornings, nights, and weekends need structure so everyone isn't running in fifty million directions and getting nowhere. When the nighttime routines are done—dinner has been eaten, baths taken, homework done, and lunches made for the next day—you can catch up on the day's events or pile into bed together.

Single-Parent Disciplining Can Be Tough

"Wait till your father gets home" is a phrase that's gone the way of the dodo bird. Dad doesn't come home anymore. And if the kids are with you for more than half the time, you're also the one who's faced with the task of disciplining errant behaviour. Even within nuclear families, women often complain that they are left the unenviable role of disciplinarian. If you're the only game in town, the job becomes even more obviously yours. And now you don't even have the option of buying time with the standard, "I'll talk it over with your father." Instead, you get to make a unilateral decision that your kids will automatically resent—yum.

Not unfamiliar is the story of single parent struggling on a tight budget while the non-custodial parent spends lavishly on the children when they visit. While you're pleased that your kids have had a wonderful time, you want to cry because you're always the one who has to say no, be sensible, watch the pennies. You would love to spoil your kids too, and can't bear to see Daddy getting all the glory when you seem to be facing all the responsibility alone.

But being the disciplinarian doesn't have to be all bad. And while watching the other guy be the Disney dad can be hard, you don't have to let it diminish what you do have with your kids. Children need more than stuff. People need more than stuff. At the end of a life, it is not the one with the most toys who wins; it is the one with the most love whose soul may soar untethered.

So you're in charge—alone. Even if you have a good co-parenting relationship with your ex, when the homework, the dishes, the vacuuming has to be done in your house, you've got to be the one that makes it happen. First up, give yourself permission to be in charge. You are responsible for these children. It is up to you to impart the values, wisdom, and life skills they'll need to survive. As a loving, strong, and supportive parent, you have the right to tell them what to do. And you have the right to expect your children to obey you.

Of course that means you actually have to tell them what you want them to do. A wishy-washy "Gosh, I could really use some help cleaning up" won't get anywhere the same kind of positive response as a sturdy "Alexandra, I'm washing the dishes, come and dry please." It's all a matter of confidence. Some people call those optional statements—"You shouldn't playing with that," or "Don't you think we should be getting ready for bed?"—cooperative parenting. But if it was cooperative, then the kids would be cooperating. Fact is, kids don't get the subtlety of this type of request. You need to be focussed and direct: "John, that's not a toy. Put it down, " and "Okay kids, it's bedtime. Turn off the television now."

Don't get trapped into repeating yourself over and over and over and over. It's a kid ploy to buy time; and it seriously counters the validity of whatever it is you're trying to get accomplished. If you have to turn purple and pound the table to get your kids to do anything, then you're not using the only-say-it-once rule. Make a clear statement of what you want done. If it doesn't happen, let there be an immediate consequence that's related to the issue.

When my daughter was only three or so, the Tidy Monster started to visit our house. I recall the impetus for his first visit. As Alexandra was headed up the stairs, I called to her, "You've left your crayons all over the carpet. Please come and clean them up."

"No," she said, as she kept heading up the stairs.

"Well, don't blame me if the Tidy Monster comes and takes them away then," I responded mysteriously. It was a stroke of genius. That night I cleaned up the crayons and put them in a high cupboard. The next morning Alexandra wanted to know where they were. "I guess the Tidy Monster did come after all," I said.

"What do you mean? What's the Tidy Monster?" she asked, with a tremble on her lip.

"Well, when you leave your stuff all over the place, the Tidy Monster comes and takes it away."

"Does he ever bring it back?"

"If you keep your toys neat and tidy, he might. He wants to see that you really do value them."

"If he doesn't bring it back, what does he do with it?"

"I guess he might give it to a little boy or girl who isn't as lucky as you and doesn't have as much stuff. They would take good care of it."

Within three days the Tidy Monster had brought back the crayons. And from time to time, when everything was in order, the Tidy Monster would leave a gift on Alexandra's bed. She would run yelling into my office, "Mommy, the Tidy Monster brought me a present. I've been so good and keeping my stuff neat that he gave me these stickers."

My daughter is six now, and the Tidy Monster still comes from time to time. But not nearly as much as in those early years when she was testing the limits.

If you have older children and they've already learned to ignore you, it may take more proving before they believe that you're not about to continue in the old ways. Hang in there. Be consistent. It's definitely worth the effort.

Children have an extraordinary ability to pinpoint their parent's weak spots. They take those areas of weakness and worry at them, like a dog gnaws at a bone, until your resolve is weakened and you simply give in. Tired, worn down, and for no good reason, you reverse your original decision. Watch out! Here comes trouble. Now you're on the "Oh, mom doesn't really mean it when she says that" merry-go-round. If your kids start in with the nagging, the begging, the threats of removing their love forever and maybe even longer, disengage. Walk away. Show your child that you will not be persuaded by such negative persistence

Ultimately, you'll get what you want from your children by giving them what they want most from you—your time. A little time every day, an always attentive ear, and lots of praise and encouragement will help you create a bond of trust and loyalty with your kids. And don't forget to tell them you love them. Yes, you can nag…as long as the words are "I love you."

Making It Through the Holidays

Since the holidays tend to be chock full of family associations and memories, they can be really tough on you, at least until you've established new rituals. Even people who are not living through transition experience a sense of letdown after the holidays. So if you're blue, cut yourself some slack. It's to be expected.

New traditions need to be established. You and your children can redefine your roles for the holidays. Shop together, decorate your home, or make a gift for the local bazaar. While you're moving about your life, setting new goals and creating new memories, talk. Tell your kids it's okay to be a little sad for things that have gone, and let yourself be a little sad, too. Talk about the memories you have of holidays past. Cry. Release the yesterdays so you can make space for your tomorrows.

Invite friends and family to attend your First Annual Official Whatever Party. Everyone can bring a homemade decoration to help you get started with your new holiday traditions. Or make it a pot-luck dinner. You may not be joyous on your first forays into your new traditions but, if you create an atmosphere of warmth and love, you will begin to heal.

Get together with other single parents and talk about the challenges and the creative solutions you've found for dealing with them. Keep your schedule simple but sufficiently full to help you stay connected with the spirit of the season.

If your children will be spending part of the holidays with their father, make plans to visit with friends and family. No one close by? Consider a community project, which involves you in giving to others.

While you will feel nostalgic for the old days, and a little sad about being alone during the holidays, don't make your kids feel guilty about leaving you all alone, by yourself, with no one to talk to. Encourage them to have a great time. Tell them what your plans are so they can see that you won't be sitting at home moping alone.

DDDDating!

You can date. You can not-date. You can say you're not dating while you date, or that you are dating when you are not. Those are the options available, and you're going to have to choose the one that works best for you. Some people want to start rebuilding their lives quickly and look for new opportunities to form intimate relationships. Then there are those who for various reasons will not put themselves back out on the line: they're waiting for their children to be grown; they don't want to be hurt again; they don't want anyone else coming into their lives and telling them how to live. And then there are the people who claim that every man they go out with is just a friend. They don't want to signal to their children or their exes that they are moving to a new stage of life. Perhaps they like playing the wounded wife, and a new man would give them less reason to complain. Or perhaps they are worried about introducing a new man into the lives of their family and friends without being sure how long he'll stay.

Diana's Story

I always told myself it would take me two years to get over it. People kept saying, "You've got to get out there, you've got to start meeting other guys." But I couldn't for the first year. Then for the second year, it was "God, I really have to accept the fact that I'm a single person" because we'd been a couple for so long, for my whole adult life we'd been a couple, that it was just so shocking that now I have to been just me. Things like marriage are just so defining. I was known as Justin's wife and we were a couple.

I leave the experience a little sadder because I am more aware of what that loneliness or that hurt feels like. That's what it is, it's rejection and it's hurt and then it's loneliness because you are with someone for so long and you are together all the time. You sleep together every night and then all of a sudden there is no one in your bed. And you come home and the house is exactly as you left it that morning and it's quiet and empty and you feel so, so lonely.

I don't think that I am as far along as I'd like to be. I don't know how to get over this. You put a lot of pressure on yourself to get on with it. I recently went on a few dates with a guy and he wasn't for me and that's fine. But he was a very nice guy and I think that one of the things he started to do was to restore my faith. But I couldn't help but think of Justin and compare him to Justin. But it was a good experience for me because I know that getting into the next one will be better. Now I feel like on an intellectual level I'm ready to date.

My Dad told me I needed to take the subway because I could meet somebody on the subway. I said, "Dad, that is absurd." He said, "You get in your car and you go to work, you get in your car and you go to the gym, you get in your car and you go home. And that's this triangle that you go through every day." I stepped back from that and thought, "You know what? Not that going on the subway is the answer, but he's right." I am insulated and I've got this routine. I really should broaden out a little bit more, do different things and go different places.

> When I was married, I used to think that there were a lot of guys out there for me. But that was when I was married and I had a smile. I think I'm not as attractive as I used to be because I've got this sadness.

Of course, the mere thought of dating at this point may be more than you can emotionally cope with. If you're still in your I-hate-men-all-men-but-most-especially-my-husband stage, perhaps you should hold off for a while. No guy wants to sit and listen to you babble on about what a jerk your ex is, how you got screwed, and just how stupid his new wife is. If you're still bleeding, you need to wait a while longer.

If you're from the school of I'll-never-date-as-long-as-my-children-are-home, you have to ask yourself if your isolation is good for either you or your children. Relationships do bring sadness, but they also bring great joy. And to deny yourself and your children the opportunity to form new friendships could be a mistake. Think of dating as your opportunity to show your kids how relationships work amongst functional and healthy grownups. You want them to know that not everyone is a keeper, that it takes time to create strong bonds, and that if things just don't work out, you can end the relationship sanely, albeit sadly. Don't underestimate the importance of your children seeing that you have a life. They'll feel less guilty as they walk down the street with their friends because they don't need to tend to Mom. She can take care of herself. And hey, she's having a good time too.

Ever Heard of the Transitional Relationship?

When I ended my second marriage, almost immediately I entered a relationship with a man with whom I had worked. He was a nice man, and he was smitten. Since my ex hadn't appeared to be smitten for some time before I left, it was very satisfying being with someone who really liked spending time with me. But there was no doubt in my mind, from the get-go, that this was no more than a transitional relationship.

What the dickens is a transitional relationship? It's one that you have no intention of maintaining long term—one that serves your immediate needs, gets you through, makes you feel beautiful, provides you with much-needed practice in doing boy-girl things (as opposed to the husband-wife things you've been doing). One from which you expect no commitment; one to which you do not intend to commit.

Watch out! If you're not aware of the transitional relationship you can be hurt.

> ## Cynthia's Story
>
> When Paul walked into my life, I was sure he was the perfect man. My judgement was all off. Because Frank (my ex) hadn't paid much attention to how I looked or what I thought for a long time, Paul's attention seemed to be that much more magical. I felt that we had a lot in common. When he stopped calling I was crestfallen. I figured I must be some kind of awful person for this to happen twice in succession. It wasn't to be the last time either. Until I got my dating legs back, I had a really hard time telling the gems from the jerks and I paid the price with my self-esteem.

You may be looking for or latching on to a transitional relationship, but you can do a lot of damage if you aren't aware of what's going on and aren't completely honest about it. You need to let your new partner know that he's the first guy back on the pony, so to speak. He needs to be aware that you're going through a transition, and that he may very well be no more that a prescription.

If you end up being some other person's transitional woman, you might think he's in love with you, when in fact he's just in love with the whole feeling of being in love. It isn't you, *per se*; it could be anybody (sorry). And you need to know this before you pour your heart and soul into the relationship, particularly if it's an early relationship after you've become single again.

Mothers Who Work

Did you know that more than 70 percent of married women with children under 16 are employed?[1] Surprised? What's probably more surprising is that this figure is higher than the 61 percent of lone mothers with kids under 16 who work outside the home. And I've got another surprising statistic for you: while 47 percent of single moms with kids under six are working, that's 20 percent fewer than their married counterparts.

When I went looking for the research on working single moms, I never expected to find the incidence of working mothers to be higher for dual-parent families than for single parents. The harried single mom rushing from work to daycare and home again, juxtaposed with the calm and in-control stay-at-home married mother, is one of the myths that seems to continue to hold water, despite all that's been written about the changing face of Canadian families.

As a working single mother, don't allow yourself to be saddled with the destructive myths of the working mother. You do not have to be a stay-at-home mother to be a good mom. Happily employed mothers have self-confidence and can use their experiences to boost their children's self-esteem—after all, kids learn all about self-esteem by identifying with the strong adult influences in their families.

Above all, it is the quality of the relationship you have with your children that will count the most. As a happy and fulfilled woman, you're likely to be a happy mother. Your family isn't deficient simply because it is headed by a single parent, any more than it is deficient because it is headed by a woman. Two parents under one roof is no assurance that harmony and love will prevail.

Of course, you may not have had to consider child-care options as an at-home mom. Now, as a working mom, child care will be a primary concern. The relationship between your children and their child-care provider is an important one. Qualities to look include

- a good match between your child's temperament and needs, and the caregiver's ability to meet them

- a low ratio of children to caregiver in a group-care situation

- the potential for a strong on-going relationship between your child and the caregiver—shown by low turnover

- caregiver training in health, safety, and child development

Spend some time watching how your child interacts with the caregiver. Drop by unannounced to see how it's going. As much as you can, participate in your child's daycare experience: bake cupcakes for a special party, or make decorations for an upcoming event. Develop an open and honest communication. Watch for the new skills your child is bringing home. And check with your child regularly to see how safe he or she feels, and how much fun he or she is having.

Give your child a number to call you during the day for emergencies, or just to chat about how the day went. Create routines so you know what your child is doing and your child knows what you're doing; it'll help you both to feel connected to each other. Bring your child to work, to see you in your environment. Save 15 to 25 minutes per day for a back-rub, foot massage, or hair-brushing. As you relax together, you'll be surprised what you'll hear and how connected you'll feel.

You can do a great job of balancing your job and your kids, as long as you don't allow those cultural myths to undermine your confidence. If you feel guilty about the amount of time you have to spend at work, give your head a shake. Or find a new job. Stop feeling guilty. You're not only not to blame for all the things that go wrong in your kids' lives, you're also the reason why so much goes right. Give yourself a little credit.

Changing Your Name

I know women who have divorced and immediately changed their names—some to their maiden names, some to a totally new name of their own creation. There's a sense that they have reverted to their pre-marriage innocence or reinvented themselves. In their book, *The Language of Names*, Justin Kaplan and Anne Bernays demonstrate again and again how the taking of a new name creates a genuine sense of change for the personality involved.

But before you go rushing out to change your name, keep in mind that you'll likely be creating a tonne of work for yourself. Aside from the legal issues, you'll also have to change your name on your driver's license, credit cards, health card, passport, voter registration, club and association memberships, school forms, medical records…the list goes on and on.

According to the law, you can call yourself whatever name you want, so long as you are not using a new name for an illegal purpose, such as avoiding your debts, pretending you are someone else, or hiding from the police. So you can, in fact, use a name that is different from your legal name without doing anything. If you want to change your name officially so that the name you use every day is your legal name, you have to apply to the Registrar General of Ontario.

You can change your legal name for all sorts of reasons: to change the spelling of your name so people find it easier to write and pronounce, or to make your nickname your legal name. Perhaps you want kids to have the same last name as their step-parent. As long as you can come up with a legitimate reason, you won't have any trouble getting your name changed.

If you try to change your name because of a marriage or common-law relationship, you'll only be allowed to change your surname. Do it within 90 days of your marriage and there is no fee.

At the end of your marriage or common-law relationship—through separation, divorce or death—you can change your legal name back to what it was before. You have to complete a new application form within 90 days of the end of your relationship.

To get an application and information booklet, call the Registrar General at 1-800-461-2156. Then send in the completed application form, the necessary certified copies (a photocopy won't cut it), and the application fee. The Registrar General's staff will check to make sure everything is hunky-dory and will send you a change-of-name certificate showing your new legal name. Your new name is now your legal name. The whole process takes about two months.

Staying in Touch with Far-Away Children

If you're the one that moved far away, or if subsequent to your divorce one or more of your children move quite some distance to their father's house, you'll have to learn to manage your relationship from afar. This isn't easy, but it can be done. With a little time and effort, you can stay connected to your child. Whether you share your love of movies by writing reviews of flicks you've seen and sending them to your child, or take out a subscription to your child's hometown newspaper so you can see what's going on nearby, staying in your child's life should be more than just the visits you coordinate each year.

Perhaps the most important rule for long-distance parenting is to keep your promises. If you've been planning a camping trip together, it doesn't matter how important that business contract is, you must keep your word to your child. Don't let your guilt over the divorce tempt you to make grand promises you won't or can't keep. While you may find it easy to forget what you've promised, your child will be living for the moment that the promise comes true. So only promise when you know for dead certain you can deliver.

The second most important rule may be to stay connected: telephone, letters, and e-mail are all ways of staying in your child's life. Does this sound obvious? It's amazing how many far-away parents don't write or call often enough. As time goes by and their children's lives change, they have no idea what's going on.

Faith's Story

When Karl moved away with the kids I thought that my heart would break. I was doing so well up until then, and suddenly I couldn't see the boys anymore. I was determined to stay in their lives. So I started writing letters. I'd write a page each day, and as soon as I got a letter from them I'd post mine. They picked up on it and started doing it too. So it was like writing a diary to each other. When they came for visits with me, it was like we hadn't been apart at all because I knew everything that was going on in their lives. Maybe even more than Karl. And because I wasn't there being the disciplinarian all the time, the boys felt they could tell me anything. It wasn't perfect, but we made the best of it.

The caveat here is to remember that your children need to be your children, not your pals. So be careful when talking about your romantic relationships, your concerns, your finances, or any other problems you're facing. Focus on the things your children will love to read about. Share your ideas and your feelings; don't just use your kids as your confessors.

Take lots of pictures and include them in your correspondence. And tell them where you've put the pictures, arts and crafts, anything they've sent you; take a picture of the treasure in your home and send that along to show what your life looks like.

Call as often as you can afford to, so you can hear their voices and they yours. When you do call, check to make sure it's a good time, that they're not sitting down to supper or in the middle of homework. This is even more important if you're calling on a special occasion, when the kids might be torn in their loyalties between you and your spouse or his new wife. If you can, set a specific time when you'll call and stick to it; that way the kids will know when to expect to hear from you.

The more you know about your child's life, the closer your long-distance relationship will be. Make sure the school sends you copies of everything your spouse gets. You might want to pick up a copy of one of your child's textbooks, or read a novel they're doing at school, so you can talk about it or check his or her progress. When you travel to your child's neck of the woods, meet teachers, friends, the swim instructor. Whatever is important to your child should be important to you, so submerge yourself in your child's life.

Try to keep the things you shared a special interest in alive for both of you. If you both like to watch the same television show, make a date to watch it at the same time and then chat about it when you talk on the phone or write. If you like to play chess, play a game by snail mail or e-mail. If you both love fashion, clip and send pictures from magazines.

Plan your child's visits with you well in advance, and plan them together. This lets him adjust his activities around the visits, and gives him something to look forward to. Encourage her to bring pictures of her other family so you can get to know the people in her life at home. And when he's with you, encourage him to call home. Above all, you want your child to know that you're happy when she's happy.

Perhaps the toughest thing you'll have to do to stay in your children's lives is stay in your ex's life. Since your ex is in a position to encourage or discourage your long-distance parenting, you need to have a good relationship with him. If the other parent doesn't appear to want a relationship, just keep trying. Don't gush. Make it clear that, in the interest of your shared children, you want to be able to deal easily with your ex.

8

Divorced?
Finally!

You've negotiated your separation agreement, or you've been to court and had a judge make the decisions. You've established new routines for yourself and with your children. And you were just notified that your divorce is final. You take a deep breath, one filled with a sense of loss, perhaps some remaining anger, but also an overwhelming sense of relief. It's over.

Maybe. Maybe not.

If you and your ex were all there was, if you're not financially dependent, and you're both willing to go your separate ways, then it can be all over for you. And as my darling friend Scarlett said, "Thank God it's over." But if you'll be relying on your ex for income, if you have children, or if you are connected through other family members, then it'll never be over.

There will be discussions about money, about over-nights, about holidays and weekends, about what clothes the kids left where, about switching dates so the kids can see their cousins while they are in town, about how your income will be affected when he changes jobs. Then, when one or both of you remarry, you'll add the complication of new personalities into the mix. And if one of you moves, needs more money, or can't make payments, you'll be dragged back into each other's lives.

Not even the most brilliant lawyer can negotiate the perfect agreement; one that will never have to be modified. And since lawyers are only human—yes, they are—it's very likely that any agreement you've come to will be subject to interpretation. And as long as you're a living, changing person, so too will your circumstances continue to change.

Let's take child-support payments as an example. When you ventured into your divorce, you were awarded child-support payments based on the fact that you had little or less income, and that your ex was at his professional peak. Then things changed. He lost his job. You got a promotion. Guess what? You'll probably find yourself back in court on the other end of a request to have support changed. Ditto spousal support, custody, and visitation.

Since there's nothing you can do to avoid these kinds of changes, it's important to keep a cool head, and to keep contact contact with your divorce lawyer. However, wherever possible try to stay away from litigating. It's expensive and it's disruptive. If you must, you must. But if there's any other way, try that first. Mediation is perhaps the most useful tool in situations where circumstances have changed and a new set of rules must be negotiated.

In assessing whether to go back to court, it would be wise to avoid falling into the trap of laying down—or for that matter, picking up—the gauntlet, doing something for the sake of principal, fighting over a issue without first weighing how important that issue really is for both you and your ex. Since your lawyer makes money by being your knight in shining armor, he or she may be perfectly willing to ride in, armed to the teeth with your money. What you need to do—to see if the fight is worth the cost, both financially and emotionally, and to both you and your children—is to ask your lawyer how likely it is that you'll win.

Most lawyers will be pretty honest about your chances. Of course, you've got to listen and hear. It's often easy to override a lawyer's best advice in the heat of the moment. So the next question to ask your lawyer is how much this is going to cost you. You need to look at both your lawyer's fee and the costs associated with the fight.

Keep in mind that any fight you have with your spouse is going to have a long-term consequence. Your children *will* be caught in the middle. And your relationship with your ex will suffer. The longer the fight drags on, the harder it will be to repair your relationship with your ex. After all, as adversaries, you'll have little to communicate about pleasantly.

Sharon's Story

When I had to go to court with Brent over getting Jeff into a special school that could deal with his learning disability, I tried to keep it all from Jeff. But every weekend, when Jeff would go to Brent's, his father would tell him that I was causing a big upset, that I was the one creating the problems, that I was dragging him into court because I thought he (Jeff) was stupid. Finally, I put my foot down and explained what was going on to Jeff. I see now that it was a mistake to try and keep him in the dark. I didn't tell him all the dirty stuff his father had done and said. I just explained as simply as I could why he needed to go to the new school and show how important it was that we get him enrolled.

After the Divorce

Once the legal part of your divorce is over, you'll have to wrap up the financial and emotional parts. Keep meticulous records of your financial separation. Should you ever need to refer to your sep agreement or the court award, it should be readily accessible. In all likelihood you've put your financial life on hold until your divorce was finalized. Now you'll have to start planning for the future. And if you're still in agony over the divorce, you'll need to get some counselling. Don't let your anger and sadness over the ending of your relationship overflow into the child custody and money issues.

Where to begin. Well, first off, you'll want to do whatever needs to be done to transfer ownership of assets. By now you should have closed out all your jointly held accounts, credit cards, and the like. But if you haven't, get going, girl! If you've signed on a loan that your spouse has, have your name removed from the loan agreement. If you remain as a signature on the loan, you will be liable should your ex default.

Keep copies of support cheques that you send or receive. You'll have to keep the appropriate legal bodies apprised if you change addresses to keep getting your cheques on time.

It's also time to do a financial plan for the next year. You'll need to set some new goals, pay off bills outstanding from the divorce or marriage, and start a new savings program. It would also be a good idea to make note of the dates when things will change: when your son goes off to university, when you will stop receiving spousal or child support, when the house has to be sold.

When It's Time to Sell the House

If you were given a period of time during which you and your children could remain in the family home, at some point you may have to sell the house to finalize your equalization. The objective here should not be to do everything in your power to stymie the sale. You know what I mean: a messy home, difficulty being contacted, a sour-puss attitude. Rather, having reached the D-day, you should be doing everything in your power to get the best possible price for your home.

Your home, at this point, is no longer just a home, it's a commodity. While this is the place where your children have grown up, where you dreamed your dreams and saw some of them shattered, to a buyer this is a property. Make sure it's clean. Make sure it smells good. Follow your realtor's advice in getting the house ready to show, and make nice with your potential buyers.

It's important to present a united front to prospective buyers. The last thing a shopper wants to do is get in the middle of your armed conflict. Right off the bat, decide who will be dealing with the realtor and potential buyers. It may be you if you're the one still in the home. But it may be your ex if he has particular skill in this area. Also agree on who will pay for what in readying the house for sale. If the buyer wants new gutters, who will ante up in the short-term until the house closes and it can be evened out?

Here are some tips for how to make your house as appealing as possible:

- Fix anything that's broken. This doesn't mean doing a lot of expensive improvements. If you need a new roof because the old one leaks, fix it. If the flooring in your kitchen is buckling, replace it. Otherwise, if it's expensive, leave it alone.

- Repaint, if it's needed. One of the least expensive ways to fix up a house is to give it a fresh coat. Use neutral colours and you're less likely to turn people off.

- If your carpet is stained or ripped, you should probably spring for new floor covering. It's pretty hard for a couple to imagine their new baby crawling along the floor if it's covered in pee stains.

- Hire a professional cleaner to clean everything from stem to stern if you're not up to the job yourself. Try to make the house appear as light and bright as possible. Clear the counters, get rid of the clutter, put away the extra stuff that litters your home. Kitchen counters should be virtually clear—no toasters, knives, or the like. Remember that people will be opening your closets, checking under your sink, and inspecting your drawers. Get rid of the mess.

- Curb appeal—how your house looks from the street—is important. The garden should be neat and tidy, the deck should be freshly stained, the front door lock shouldn't stick, and the garbage cans should be out of sight.

I Just Can't Stop Crying

Alice's Story

When the divorce was finalized I started to cry and I couldn't stop. There was no turning back. Within weeks, Mike was remarried. I drove past the church, I was going to go in. But I just sat in the car and cried and cried. My life was over and he was having no trouble getting on with his. When he would call to speak with the kids, I'd run from the room crying. My friends tried to be patient, but I could tell they were getting tired of all my tears. I even got tired of myself. But I couldn't seem to stop crying. I felt like the hurt would never stop. It took almost five months for me to stop crying. I remember waking up one morning and thinking to myself, "I didn't cry yesterday." It wasn't the end, but it was the beginning of the end. Soon I had more no-cry days than days of crying. Now I rarely cry.

You are going to cry. It's natural. You need to grieve for the end of your relationship. You need to cry.

I remember when I left my second husband, I didn't cry. I was the leaver. I was in control. What did I have to cry about? About three months into my separation a good friend of mine said to me, "You haven't cried yet. How come?" I started to bawl. I howled. I was swept away by my disappointments, my anger at my husband's failure to keep me, my fear of the future. I wailed for hours. I don't know where it came from but, when it broke, I flooded out.

If you haven't cried yet, you should be worried. If you have, and can't stop, it may be that you haven't focussed on the divorce, preferring to assign your tears to all the other things that are wrong in your life.

One of the steps people often overlook in trying to cope with the end of a marriage is the act of celebrating the marriage. No, I'm not crazy; listen up. While you'd like to justify the end of your marriage by focussing on the problems, you're a smart girl so you can't do that. You had times in your marriage when things were really great. You loved this person. You imagined spending the rest of your life together. You have to take the time to celebrate what was good about your marriage if you want to heal. Think about what made you fall in love. What do you still admire? What did your spouse do that made you feel great? What will you miss the most?

Next comes the good-bye. In the privacy of your own home, perhaps with the help of a very dear friend, tell your spouse what he or she has meant to you. Explain how much it hurts to let go. Get specific. Then verbalize your acceptance of the end of your marriage.

Set some goals. This is not about planning your cash flow for the next five years. It's about what you want from your life in the future. It's about getting yourself back on track. It's about dreaming and wondering and anticipating. It's about making your life what you want it to be. Part of this will involve redefining yourself as the newly single woman you've become. So, what kind of person do you want to be now that you're divorced? Just think—you have to opportunity to reinvent yourself. You can change your name, move, get a new job, find a new love, travel, do absolutely anything you want. You can eat chips in bed, cake for breakfast (not too often, honey, or you'll get fat), and read for hours on end. You can dye your hair, shorten your skirts, or buy a seriously sexy outfit to cook dinner in for your children. You can have it all. All you have to decide now is what you want.

Epilogue:
The End and the Beginning

Well, I've given you my best shot. Now it's your turn. Having read what I have to say, watched your girlfriend who was divorced last year, and listened to your mother's words of wisdom, you now have to make all the moves on your own. Divorce, like giving birth, is something that only you can do for yourself. You may have a coach telling you when to push, or a friend holding your hand while you give the Venusian death grip. But ultimately, when that little ol' piece of paper arrives, you'll be all on your own.

Whatever you do, while you go through the process, don't give up control of your divorce—not even to your well-spoken and dapper lawyer. Yes, your lawyer is a professional, trained to represent your interests in court. And yes, you do have to listen carefully to his or her advice. But it's not your lawyer's divorce. It's yours.

I remember when one of my lawyers first told me that the financial settlement for which I was asking wasn't sufficient to give him room to negotiate. I said it didn't matter, that there was no negotiation. See, I knew my STBE would be prepared to argue me into the dust. I'd listen to him brag about how he'd done that to his first wife. I wasn't prepared to go that route. I knew what I was legally entitled to. I also knew what I was morally entitled to. That's what I asked for. And that's what my STBE gave to me. Yes, he squawked at first, but just for a minute. Then he was a pussycat. My lawyer wondered what I had done to make him so agreeable. I knew that I had simply asked for what was fair. My ex-husband was nothing if not fair, providing you didn't infuriate him.

It's your divorce. The lawyer works for you. You get to call the shots.

Before you do, make sure you're completely informed. Trying to divvy up the property before you've completed a thorough inventory is a sure way to

- ask for too much because you don't know how little you have, or

- not ask for enough because you're unaware of what that old dog has been burying in the backyard.

While you want to get as much information as you can before you sit down to negotiate, letting too much time pass and spending too much money in the name of gathering information is a waste. Try to do it without involving the legal system, by exchanging information or using a mediator. If you're sure he's holding out on you, then you can turn back to the legal system for help.

When it comes time to negotiate your settlement, don't forget to get the advice of a tax expert. Remember those contingent liabilities Having survived the storm of your divorce, the last thing you need is to have a huge tax bill at the end of your rainbow.

Of course, while you're going through the motions of divorce, you'll also be riding an emotional roller coaster. Don't let anyone try to tell you what you need to do, or how you should be feeling. This is your divorce, and no one else can know how you feel. Rely on your intuition, that little voice inside your head. It usually knows what it's talking about.

Take care of yourself. Divorce equals stress. Stress equals ill health. This may be just the time to get an exercise routine, make a new meal plan, or start meditating. If you have children, you'll also have to watch carefully for signs of their stress, so you can talk about it and look for ways to overcome it together.

You will come through this in one piece. You won't ever be the same person you were before the divorce. But you might be a better person; or you could be a miserable, bitter, sad, and lonely person. It's your choice. It's your life. You get to decide.

Good luck. I hope you learn as much from your divorce as I learned from mine.

And keep the faith. After three tries I've finally got it right.

Endnotes

1   So, You're Getting a Divorce

1. Whitehead, Barbara Dafoe, *The Divorce Culture,* Alfred A. Knopf, Inc., p. 4.

2. Finnie, Ross, "The Economics of Divorce," in *Family Matters: New Policies for Divorce, Lone Mothers, and Child Poverty*, C.D. Howe Institute, Toronto, 1995, p. 111.

3. Turcotte, Pierre, and Belanger, Alain, "The Dynamics of Formation and Destruction of First Common-Law Unions in Canada," Statistics Canada, 1998.

4. Ahrons, Constance, *The Good Divorce: Keeping Your Family Together When Your Marriage Comes Apart,* HarperCollins, 1994, p. 12.

5. Department of Justice, *Evaluation of the Divorce Act, Phase II: Monitoring and Evaluation,* Canada: Bureau of Review, 1990.

2   The Emotional Divorce

1. Roiphe, Anne, "A Tale of Two Divorces" in Kaganoff, Penny, and Spano, Susan *Women on Divorce*, Harcourt Brace & Company, 1995, p. 23.

2. Stewart, Abigail, et al., *Separating Together: how divorce transforms families,* The Guildford Press, 1997, p. 69.

3. Stewart, Abigail, et al., *Separating Together: how divorce transforms families*, The Guildford Press, 1997, p. 66.

3   For the Sake of the Children

1. Walerstein, Judith S., and Blakeslee, Sandra, *Second Chances: Men, Women and Children a Decade after Divorce*, Thicknor & Fields, 1989, p. xiv.

2. Stewart, Abigail, et al., *Separating Together: how divorce transforms families*, The Guildford Press, 1997, p. 233.

3. Stewart, Abigail, et al., *Separating Together: how divorce transforms families*, The Guildford Press, 1997, p. 233.

4. Whitehead, Barbara Dafoe, *The Divorce Culture*, Alfred A. Knopf, Inc., p. 97

5. Stewart, Abigail, et al., *Separating Together: how divorce transforms families*, The Guildford Press, 1997, p. 236

6. American Academy of Pediatrics, "The Pediatrician's Role in Helping Children and Families Deal with Divorce," policy statement, November 1983.

7. American Academy of Pediatrics, "The Pediatrician's Role in Helping Children and Families Deal with Separation and Divorce," policy statement, July 1994.

8. Report of the Special Joint Committee on Child Custody and Access, http://www.parl.gc.ca/InfoComDoc/36/1/SJCA/Studies/Reports/sjcarp02-e.htm

4   Women, Divorce, and the Money

1. Riessman, Catherine Kohler, *Divorce Talk: Men and Women Make Sense of Personal Relationships*, New Brunsick, N.J.., Rutgers University Press, 1990, p. 165.
2. Riessman, Catherine Kohler, *Divorce Talk: Men and Women Make Sense of Personal Relationships*, New Brunsick, N.J.., Rutgers University Press, 1990, p. 165.

5   Non-Traditional Families

1. "Report on the demographic situation in Canada," *The Daily*; Statistics Canada, March 25, 1997.
2. Turcotte, Pierre, and Belanger, Alain; "The Dynamics of Formation and Destruction of First Common-Law Unions in Canada," Statistics Canada, 1998.

7   Flying Solo

1. *Canada's Families—They Count*, the Vanier Institute of the Family, 1997.

Appendix A: Resources

If you're like me, one book isn't enough. Here I've gathered a list of titles that you may find useful. It is only a guide, since many of these books came by word of mouth and I have not read them all. But I have tried to construct a list of books that covers as many of the variables as possible. Since writing style is so personal—there are books I absolutely love that others just don't get—I've tried to keep the descriptions impartial.

Books for Preschoolers

TAXI TAXI by Cari Best (Orchard Books, 1997). This story features a young Latina girl whose parents don't live together. Every Sunday, her father comes to visit in his bright yellow taxi.

THE DINOSAURS DIVORCE, by Laurene and Marc Brown (Little Brown, 1986). Direct and lively text and illustrations deal with visitation, the whys of divorce, and telling friends.

TWO HOMES TO LIVE IN: A CHILD'S-EYE VIEW OF DIVORCE, by Barbara Hazen (Human Sciences Press, 1978). Written in gentle and understandable prose, this story of a young girl whose father moves out emphasizes that she did not cause the divorce, and helps her to understand her reunion fantasy, her parents fighting, and missing her daddy.

IT'S NOT YOUR FAULT, KOKO BEAR, by Vicki Lansky (Book Peddlers, 1998). Koko Bear learns what divorce means, how to deal with changes, how to recognize and deal with feelings, and that divorce is not Koko's fault. Includes tips for parents.

WHEN DADDY COMES TO VISIT, by Maggie Burke (Winston-Derek Pub., 1997). A story in rhyme about the imaginary games a child plays when his father visits on Sundays.

DADDY, by Jeannette Caines (Harper and Row, 1977). A story about the joys of a child's visits with her father and stepmother each Saturday. The loving and caring relationships portrayed in this African-American stepfamily illustrates that children continue to be loved after divorce and remarriage.

WHERE IS DADDY? THE STORY OF DIVORCE, by Beth Goff (Beacon Press, 1969). This is the story of Janeydear whose parents divorce, how she begins to understand her feelings of confusion and fear, and how she resolves them. Her parents fight; her dad moves out and her mom goes to work. By the end of the book Janeydear has begun to adjust to her new life.

MARTHA'S NEW DADDY, by Danielle Steel (Delacorte, 1989). A story about a child's feelings about remarriage. While acknowledging feelings of loss, confusion, and fear, it offers reassurance and hope.

DADDY'S ROOMMATE by Michael Willhoite (Horn Book, Inc., 1991). This young boy's story begins with his parents' divorce and continues with the arrival of "someone new at Daddy's house." He discusses his father's new living situation, in which the father and his gay roommate share eating, doing chores, playing, loving and living.

MOM AND DAD DON'T LIVE TOGETHER ANY MORE, by Kathy Stinsonn (Firefly, 1984). Soft watercolors illustrate this little girl's description of her family's transition to joint custody parenting.

WHO WILL LEAD THE KIDDISH? by Barbara Pomerantz (UAHC, 1985). This is the story of a young Jewish girl adjusting to her parents' divorce. She spends Shabbat at her father's apartment, where he gives her a Kiddish cup to take home.

Books for Elementary Schoolers

WHY ARE WE GETTING A DIVORCE? by Peter Mayle (Crown, 1978/88). This book humorously and sensitively covers many difficult issues with objectivity. It looks at why people get married and have children, and how some parents come to the decision to divorce. It offers ideas about reorganizing the family, and encourages children to have empathy for their parents, and to take responsibility for helping with household chores and caring for themselves.

I WISH I HAD MY FATHER, by Norma Simon (Albert Whitman, 1983). A good book for children who struggle with the feelings of rejection and sadness caused by a parent who has left them.

PLEASE COME HOME, by Doris Sanford (Multnomeh Press, 1985). An eight-year-old wonders what will happen to her now that Daddy has gone. Her teddy bear comforts her, and she learns to feel okay by herself.

PRICILLA TWICE, by Judith Caseley (Greenwillow Books, 1995). The story of a girl who feels split in half. It helps children understand in reassuring and even humorous ways that there is more than one kind of family.

DEAR MR. HENSHAW, by Beverly Cleary (Avon Co., 1994). An award winning book about a ten-year-old boy who writes letters to an unmet hero describing how he misses his father.

MY MOTHER'S HOUSE, MY FATHER'S HOUSE, by C.B. Christiansen, (Atheneum, 1989). Recommended for younger elementary-school-aged children who spend part of the week with each parent, it is about a child's experience of living in two homes.

MEGAN'S BOOK OF DIVORCE, by Erica Jong (New American Library, 1984). Precocious four-year-old Megan tells her side of the story of her parents' separation and her enlightened joint-custody situation. Each parent has a significant other.

MY LIFE TURNED UPSIDE DOWN, BUT I TURNED IT RIGHT-SIDE UP, by Mary Blitzer Field and Hennie Share (Child Works Child Play, 1994). The story of how a young girl handles the challenges of living in two places.

TWO PLACES TO SLEEP, by Joan Schuchman (Carol-Rhoda Books, 1979). The story of seven-year-old David, who lives with his father in their original house and visits his mother in her apartment on weekends. It emphasizes his happiness with each parent, that he is loved as much as ever, and that the divorce is not his fault.

AT DADDY'S ON SATURDAYS, by Linda Girard (Albert Whitman, 1988). After Katie's parents divorce, her daddy moves away. Saturdays seem far away, but her mother and her teacher help her through the week until Saturday, when she does see her father.

Preteen- and Teenage-Appropriate Books

HOW IT FEELS WHEN PARENTS DIVORCE, by Jill Krementz (Knopf, 1984). Twenty girls and boys, aged 7 to 16, express their feelings about their parents' divorces. They talk about their feelings, the good and bad parts of joint custody, and the adjustments they must make when their parents begin to date or remarry.

IT'S NOT THE END OF THE WORLD, by Judy Blume (Bradbury Press, 1972). The story of how three siblings react to their parents' separation. Karen, the middle child, is concerned about how the family will manage financially and who will take care of them. She tries to get her parents to reconcile. Her six-year-old sister develops fears of the dark and of being left alone. Her fourteen-year-old brother runs away for a few days.

Karen meets another girl whose parents are divorced and learns some new ways of coping from her.

THE BOYS AND GIRLS BOOK ABOUT DIVORCE, by Richard A. Gardner, M.D. (Bantam, 1971). Gardner clearly understands the concerns of children, and talks to them in a language they can relate to. The emphasis is on what children and adolescents can do to help themselves.

THE KIDS' GUIDE TO DIVORCE, by J. Brogan and U. Maiden (Fawcett, 1986). Discusses the practical issues that affect children.

WHAT'S GOING TO HAPPEN TO ME?, by Edna LeShan (Macmillan, 1978). Discusses joint custody, the value of family therapy, and how to retain a belief in marriage.

THE DIVORCE EXPRESS, by Paula Danziger (Delacorte, 1982). Fourteen-year-old Phoebe spends weekdays with her father in the suburbs and commutes back to the city to be with her mother for weekends on a bus called the "divorce express." Just when she thinks she has a handle on it all, her mom makes a decision that will change everything again.

MY PARENTS ARE DIVORCED, TOO, by Melanie Ford, Annie and Steven Ford (Magination Press, 1997). Three stepsiblings in a blended family discuss their experiences, and those of friends, with divorce and remarriage. This is a guidebook for getting adjusted to a new life, and a means for opening new avenues of communicate at a difficult time.

WILL DAD EVER MOVE BACK HOME? by Paula Z. Hogen (Raintree Steck-Vaughn, 1995). This book presents many of the emotions experienced by children in divorcing families

A BOOK FOR JODAN, by Marcia Newfield (Atheneum, 1975). Jodan's parents separate and she moves with her mother from New York to

California. The book offers strategies for bridging long-distance parent-child relationships (letters, photos, creating a scrapbook).

STEP TROUBLE, by William L. Coleman (Comp Care Publishers, 1993). A book for older children dealing with joining a new family. Stories are told by teens, parents, stepparents, and grandparents, with suggestions about how to ease the transition.

WHEN MOM AND DAD DIVORCE, by Steven L. Nickman (Julian Messner, 1986). Addresses common fears, what happens legally in a divorce, forms of custody, parental dating, and stepfamilies. This book stresses the importance of taking advantage of available resources when times are difficult.

A SOLITARY BLUE, by Cynthia Voigt (Atheneum, 1983). A sophisticated story about a high-school boy who resolves his feelings about his custodial father and absent mother. Jeff's mother, who deserted the family years before, re-enters his life and challenges Jeff to overcome his pain about his family.

Books for Adults

THE GOOD DIVORCE, by Constance Ahrons, Ph.D. (HarperPerennial, 1994).

HELPING YOUR KIDS COPE WITH DIVORCE THE SANDCASTLES™ WAY, by M. Gary Neuman, LMHC, with Patricia Romanowski (Times Books, Random House, 1998).

HOW TO SURVIVE THE LOSS OF A LOVE, by Colgrove, et al. (Prelude Press, 1993).

BREAKING UP: From Heartache to Happiness in 48 Pages, by Y. Nave (Workman).

VICKI LANSKY'S DIVORCE BOOK FOR PARENTS: Helping your Children Cope with Divorce and its Aftermath, by Vicki Lansky (Signet, 1991).

HELPING CHILDREN COPE WITH SEPARATION AND LOSS, by C. Jewitt Jarratt (Harvard Common, 1994).

101 WAYS TO BE A LONG DISTANCE SUPER-DAD, by George Neuman (Blossom Valley Press, 1983)

LONG DISTANCE PARENTING by Miriam Galper Cohen (NAL, 1989).

WHOSE CHILD CRIES? Children of Gay Parents Talk About Their Lives, by Joe Gantz (Jalmar Press, 1983).

GAY PARENTING: A Complete Guide for Gay Men and Lesbians with Children, by Joy Schulenburg (Doubleday Anchor, 1985).

FROM WEDDED WIFE TO LESBIAN LIFE: Stories of Transformation, by Deborah Abbott & Ellen Farmer (Crossing Press, 1995).

THE OTHER SIDE OF THE CLOSET: The Coming-Out Crisis for Straight Spouses and Families, by Amity Pierce Buxton (Wiley, 1994).

MARRIED WOMEN WHO LOVE WOMEN, by Carren Strock (Doubleday, 1998).

STRENGTHENING YOUR STEPFAMILY, Elizabeth Einstein and Linda Albert (American Guidance Service, 1986).

STEPFAMILY REALITIES, Margaret Newman (New Harbinger Publications, 1994).

Child-Support Guidelines Resources

Call the Department of Justice toll-free number for child support publications: 1-888-373-2222. Or visit The Department of Justice website: www.canada.justice.gc.ca

Alberta
Queen's Bench Child Support Center
Calgary 297-6600
Edmonton 415-0404
Operator 310-0000

British Columbia
1-888-216-2211
Vancouver 660-2192

Manitoba
Child Support Resource Centre 1-877-943-2631
Winnipeg 1-204-945-2631
Manitoba has child support guidelines under the Family Maintenance Act as of June 1, 1998. The Manitoba guidelines also apply to cases under the Divorce Act where both parents reside in Manitoba.

New Brunswick
1-888-236-2444

Newfoundland
1-709-729-1831
The Province of Newfoundland has not yet amended the Family Law Act to incorporate child support guidelines.

Nova Scotia

1-800-665-9779

Halifax 455-3135

N.W.T.

1-800-661-0798

Callers should indicate that they would like to speak to someone regarding the Federal Child Support Guidelines.

Ontario

1-800-980-4962

On December 1, 1997, the Ontario government passed a bill that brings Ontario's Family Law Act into line with the federal government's Child Support Guidelines. For further information on the Ontario Child Support Guidelines, you may access the Ministry of the Attorney General website: www.attorneygeneral.jus.gov.on.ca/serfjm.htm

Prince Edward Island

1-800-240-9798

Quebec

Communication Québec 1-800-363-1363

Quebec Justice Department 1-418-643-5140

The Province of Quebec has provincial guidelines that came into force on May 1, 1997.

Saskatchewan

1-888-218-2822

Saskatchewan adopted the Federal Child Support Guidelines as of May 1, 1997.

Yukon

1-800-661-0408

Whitehorse 667-5437

Canada Pension Plan

To request a credit split or more information about the Canada Pension Plan, please call Human Resources Development Canada free of charge:
1-800-277-9914 English
1-800-277-9915 French

Finding Parenting Help on the Net

ParentLink

1-800-552-8522. Provides research-based information to assist parents.

Focus on Kids

Provides linkages to lists of books, organizations, and websites for parents. www.outreach.missouri.edu/cooper/fok/

Parents Without Partners

PWP international headquarters, 401 N. Michigan Avenue, Chicago, IL 60611 (312-644-6610). Provides free referrals to local PWP chapters, which offer social and educational opportunities for single parents. Membership fees vary. www.parentswithoutpartners.org

Single Parent Resource Center

31 E. 28th Street, Suite 200, New York, NY 10016-9998 (212-951-7030). Offers information about how to start a single-parent support group. www.singleparentresources.com

National Organization of Single Mothers, inc.

P.O. Box 68, Midland, NC 28107 (704-888- 5437). Provides free advice on how to start support. Publishes *Single Mother* magazine (bi-monthly). One-year individual membership: $12.97 US. www.singlemothers.org

The Stepfamily Association of America, Inc.

650 J Street, Suite 205, Lincoln, NE 68508 (1-800-735-0329). Publishes a quarterly magazine, *Stepfamilies*, and an 89-page book, *Stepfamilies Stepping Ahead*. Provides referrals to more than 60 local chapters nationwide. Offers a variety of hard-to-find books, tapes, manuals, and other materials about stepfamilies. One-year membership, including magazine subscription and book: $35. www.stepfam.org

The Stepfamily Network, Inc.

555 Bryant Street #361, Palo Alto, CA 94301 (1-800-487-1073). Provides information on stepfamily resources and support groups. It is a non-profit organization dedicated to helping stepfamily members achieve harmony and mutual respect. stepfamily.net

The Stepfamily Foundation

333 West End Avenue, New York, NY 10023 (212-877-3244). Publishes lists of books, audio tapes and video tapes for stepfamilies. One-year membership: $70. www.stepfamily.org

The Straight Spouse Network (SSN)

www.glpci.org/~ssn/

Divorce Websites

www.divorcemag.com—*Divorce Magazine* website. Information for all States, Provinces, and territories. Subscribe to the print magazine here.

US Divorce Websites

www.divorcesupport.com
www.SmartDivorce.com/
www.divorcenet.com
www.divorcesupport.com
www.divorcehelp.com
www.divorce-online.com
www.divorcecentral.com

Canadian Divorce Websites

http://www.familylawcentre.com/famlaw.html —Joel Miller's site. Perhaps the best site in Canada.
http://www.interlog.com/~famlaw/ —Gene Colman's site. Well worth a visit.
www.home.iSTAR.ca/~dpr/ —Calgary Divorced Parents' Resources
P.O. Box 347, Station D, Calgary, Alberta, T2K 2V9 (403-275-2532, 24 hrs).

Appendix B: Divorce Petition Checklist

Here is a list of questions you're going to need to answer at some point in your divorce. You might as well get started thinking about them now. Your lawyer may have more, but these will get you off to a good start.

Let's start with questions about the kids

- Who will be the custodial or residential parent?

- What rights will the other parent have in terms of being with the children?

- If there are transportation expenses incurred, who will pay them?

- Will there be any restriction on where the custodial or residential parent may move with the children?

- How will major decisions affecting the children's health, welfare, and education be made?

If you own your home

- Will your home be sold? Will one of the parties deed his or her interest to the other?

- Will one of the parties have the right to continue to live in the home, and if so, for how long?

  - Will he or she have the right to rent any portion of the home or to allow any other person to live there? (If rent will be received, who will have the right to keep it?)

  - Will that right be affected by remarriage or living in a common-law relationship?

- If the home is to be sold, either now or in the future, how will the proceeds be split?

- If the parties cannot agree on the provisions of the sale (i.e., the selling price, private sale or multiple listing), how will this be determined?

- Who will be responsible for the ordinary maintenance and carrying charges with respect to the home until it is sold?

- Who will be responsible for major repairs and the costs of preparing the home for sale?

- If and when the home is to be sold, will either party have a first option to buy it?

- Who will be responsible for the capital gains taxes that may result from the sale of the property? Who will get the associated tax deductions, if applicable?

If you rent your home

- Who will have the right to continue to live in the home?

- Who must pay the rent and other carrying charges in the future?

- How will security deposits be split?

- Will the departing spouse be obliged to help the remaining spouse in renewing the lease if the landlord will not renew it without his or her signature?

Money owed

- What personal debts (not including business loans and the home mortgage) do the parties have?

- Who will be responsible to pay each of these debts?

Personal property

- How will the furniture, household furnishings, and other items of personal property in the marital residence be split?

- How will money in savings or chequing accounts held in either the joint or individual names of the parties be split?

- How will investments such as stocks, bonds, or other securities held in either the joint or individual names of the parties be split?

- How will items such as cars, boats, motorcycles, or other items of personal property held in either the joint or individual names of the parties be split?

- To what extent will the parties have the right to share in any pension or retirement benefits to which the other is or may be entitled?

- To what extent will one party have the right to a share in the value of any business, professional practice, royalties, or other personal property owned by the other party?

Support

- Will either party be required to financially support the other? If so, how much and for how long?

- Will either party be required to pay support to the other spouse for the children? If so, how much and for how long?

- By how much will the child-support payments be reduced when the obligation for the support of one or more of the children ends?

- Will the support payments change in the future to reflect changes in the financial circumstances of either of the parties, economic conditions, or other factors?

- Who will be entitled to claim the children as exemptions for income-tax purposes?

- Will either or both parties be obligated to pay for the post-secondary education? If so, which expenses, and to what extent?

- If those expenses are financed, who will be responsible for repayment?

- Will there be any reduction in support payments while children are attending a post-secondary institution?

Insurance

- Will either party be obligated to maintain life insurance

  - for the benefit of the other, and if so, in what amount and how long?

  - for the benefit of the children, and if so, in what amount and how long? Who will be the beneficiary of such insurance?

- Will the obligation to maintain life insurance decrease (as to amount) in the future, and if so, when and in what amount?

- Will either party be obligated to provide medical or other insurance

  - for the benefit of the other? For how long?

  - for the benefit of the children? For how long?

- Who will be responsible to pay for the children's medical, dental, drug, or hospital expenses that are not reimbursed by any insurance which either of the parties may have?

Appendix C: Federal Child Support Tables

The information in this appendix can be found at the Department of Justice Canada website at canada.justice.gc.ca/en/ps/sup/grl/glpta.html

For more information contact the Department of Justice Canada. The Department of Justice Canada has a toll-free number for information on the Guidelines. On request, we would be pleased to send you more detailed information as it becomes available. Call 1-888-373-2222. In the National Capital Region, call 946-2222. The Department of Justice Canada's Internet address is: http://canada.justice.gc.ca

How to use the simplified federal child support tables

NOTE: This document provides general information only. If you want more information contact the Department of Justice Canada. This is not a legal document. You may wish to consult a lawyer for advice on how this relates to your personal situation.

The Federal Child Support Guidelines include the rules for calculating the amount of child support, as well as a table of awards for each province and territory.

This sheet provides basic information to show how the Federal Child Support Guidelines apply in most cases. The Guidelines make the calculation of child support fair, predictable and consistent.

[Note: In certain cases, the amount of child support a court orders may be different from the amount shown on the tables because:

- there are special or extraordinary expenses (such as childcare; health expenses over $100 a year; education; extra-curricular activities);

- the court finds that the amounts determined by using the Guidelines cause undue hardship;

- parents have shared custody or access to the child at least 40% of the time;

- parents have split custody (each parent has at least one child in his or her custody);

- a child is the age of majority (18 or 19 years of age, depending on the province or territory) or over and has an ongoing need for support;

- the person paying support has an income of more than $150,000 a year;

- special provisions have been made for the child in an order or agreement.]

The following steps will help you use the tables

Step 1

Do the Federal Child Support Guidelines apply to you? As of May 1, 1997, the Federal Child Support Guidelines apply to:

- parents who want to change an existing child support order obtained under the *Divorce Act;*

- parents who will pay or receive child support further to a new child support order made under the *Divorce Act.*

  There may be exceptions—See Step 3.

Step 2

What is the total annual income, before taxes, of the person who is paying, or will pay, child support? Annual income is the money a person earns from employment and self-employment and income from investments. This includes all sources of income identified in your tax return (for example: salary, wages, commissions, UI, social assistance). If you are unsure, a T4 slip or Revenue Canada Assessment may give you an indication of annual income.

Step 3

Which tables apply to your situation?

1. Both parents live in the same province or territory. If the province or territory *does not have* its own guidelines for cases under the *Divorce Act*, use the federal tables for that province or territory. However, if the province or territory *does have* its own child support guidelines, these guide-lines will apply to cases under the *Divorce Act*.

2. The person paying support lives in a different province or territory from the person receiving support. In this case, use the federal tables for the province or territory in which the person paying support lives.

3. The person paying support lives outside Canada or the address is unknown. In this case, use the federal tables for the province or territory in which the person with custody of the child or children lives.

Step 4

How much child support should be paid? Once you have found the table you need to use, the amount of child support will be listed under the income level you identified in Step 2 and the number of children for whom you are determining child support.

Income	Monthly Award			
($)	No. of Children			
	1	2	3	4
33200	291	483	637	738
33300	291	484	639	741
33400	292	486	640	743
33500	293	487	642	746
33600	294	488	643	748
33700	295	489	645	751
33800	296	491	647	753
33900	296	492	648	756

Example (Step 4)

Ontario

Note: This table is an example only. Please be sure you refer to the tables for the province or territory where the person paying support lives. The table amounts were calculated on the basis that child support payments are no longer taxable in the hands of the receiving parent nor deductible by the paying parent.

For example, let's say the person who is paying support lives in Ontario, has an income of $33,700 a year and has two children. The amount of child support would be $489 each month.

These tables cover one to four children. If you require the tables for five or more children, please get in touch with the Department of Justice Canada.

Step 5

Can the amount be adjusted? The amount of child support may be adjusted to recognize special expenses for the child or to prevent financial hardship for a parent or child in extraordinary circumstances.

Note: This table shows amounts of child support based on income to the nearest $100. There is a mathematical formula for calculating specific child support amounts between the $100 levels. For more information, please contact the Department of Justice.

Income ($)	Monthly Award ($) No. of Children				Income ($)	Monthly Award ($) No. of Children			
	1	2	3	4		1	2	3	4
6700	0	0	0	0	12000	96	176	198	220
6800	4	4	4	4	12100	97	179	202	224
6900	9	9	10	11	12200	98	182	205	228
7000	14	15	16	17	12300	99	185	208	231
7100	19	20	22	23	12400	100	188	211	235
7200	24	25	27	29	12500	100	190	214	238
7300	29	31	33	36	12600	101	193	218	242
7400	34	36	39	42	12700	102	195	221	246
7500	39	42	45	48	12800	103	196	224	249
7600	44	47	51	54	12900	104	197	227	253
7700	49	53	57	61	13000	105	198	230	256
7800	54	58	62	67	13100	106	200	234	260
7900	58	63	68	73	13200	106	201	237	264
8000	62	67	72	78	13300	107	202	240	267
8100	62	71	76	82	13400	108	203	243	271
8200	63	74	80	86	13500	109	205	246	275
8300	64	78	84	91	13600	110	206	250	278
8400	65	81	88	95	13700	111	207	253	282
8500	66	85	92	100	13800	112	208	256	285
8600	67	89	96	104	13900	112	210	259	289
8700	68	92	100	109	14000	113	211	262	293
8800	69	96	104	113	14100	114	212	266	296
8900	69	99	108	117	14200	115	213	269	300
9000	70	102	112	121	14300	115	215	272	304
9100	71	104	114	124	14400	116	216	275	307
9200	72	106	116	126	14500	117	217	278	311
9300	73	107	118	129	14600	117	218	282	314
9400	74	109	120	131	14700	118	219	285	318
9500	75	111	122	134	14800	119	221	288	322
9600	75	112	124	136	14900	119	222	291	325
9700	76	114	126	139	15000	120	223	294	329
9800	77	115	128	141	15100	121	224	298	333
9900	78	117	130	144	15200	121	226	301	336
10000	79	119	132	146	15300	122	227	304	340
10100	80	121	135	149	15400	123	228	307	343
10200	81	124	138	153	15500	123	229	310	347
10300	81	127	142	156	15600	124	231	314	351
10400	82	130	145	160	15700	125	232	317	354
10500	83	133	148	164	15800	126	233	319	358
10600	84	136	152	168	15900	126	234	321	361
10700	85	138	155	172	16000	127	236	323	365
10800	86	141	158	175	16100	128	237	324	369
10900	87	144	162	179	16200	128	238	326	372
11000	87	147	165	183	16300	129	239	328	376
11100	88	150	168	187	16400	130	241	329	380
11200	89	153	172	190	16500	130	242	331	383
11300	90	156	175	194	16600	131	243	333	387
11400	91	159	179	198	16700	132	244	334	390
11500	92	162	182	202	16800	132	245	336	394
11600	93	165	185	206	16900	133	247	338	398
11700	93	168	189	209	17000	134	248	339	401
11800	94	171	192	213	17100	134	249	341	405
11900	95	174	195	217	17200	135	250	343	409

Income ($)	Monthly Award ($) No. of Children				Income ($)	Monthly Award ($) No. of Children			
	1	2	3	4		1	2	3	4
17300	136	252	344	412	22600	199	317	434	529
17400	136	253	346	416	22700	200	318	435	531
17500	137	254	348	419	22800	201	320	437	533
17600	138	255	349	423	22900	202	321	439	535
17700	138	257	351	427	23000	203	322	440	537
17800	139	258	353	430	23100	204	323	442	539
17900	140	259	354	433	23200	205	325	444	541
18000	140	260	356	435	23300	206	326	445	543
18100	141	262	358	437	23400	207	328	447	545
18200	142	263	360	439	23500	208	330	449	547
18300	142	264	361	441	23600	209	332	450	549
18400	143	265	363	443	23700	210	334	452	551
18500	144	266	365	445	23800	211	336	454	553
18600	144	268	366	447	23900	212	338	455	556
18700	145	269	368	449	24000	213	340	457	558
18800	146	270	370	451	24100	213	342	459	560
18900	147	271	371	453	24200	214	344	461	562
19000	148	273	373	455	24300	215	346	462	564
19100	149	274	375	457	24400	216	348	464	566
19200	151	275	376	459	24500	217	350	466	568
19300	152	276	378	461	24600	218	352	467	570
19400	154	278	380	463	24700	219	354	469	572
19500	155	279	381	465	24800	220	356	471	574
19600	157	280	383	467	24900	221	358	472	576
19700	158	281	385	469	25000	222	360	474	578
19800	160	283	386	472	25100	223	362	476	580
19900	161	284	388	474	25200	224	364	477	582
20000	163	285	390	476	25300	225	366	479	584
20100	164	286	392	478	25400	226	368	481	586
20200	166	287	393	480	25500	227	370	482	588
20300	167	289	395	482	25600	228	372	484	590
20400	169	290	397	484	25700	229	374	486	592
20500	170	291	398	486	25800	230	375	487	594
20600	172	292	400	488	25900	231	377	489	596
20700	173	294	402	490	26000	232	379	491	598
20800	175	295	403	492	26100	232	381	492	600
20900	176	296	405	494	26200	233	383	494	602
21000	178	297	407	496	26300	234	385	495	604
21100	179	299	408	498	26400	235	387	497	606
21200	181	300	410	500	26500	236	389	498	608
21300	182	301	412	502	26600	237	390	500	610
21400	184	302	413	504	26700	238	392	502	612
21500	185	304	415	506	26800	239	394	503	613
21600	187	305	417	508	26900	239	396	505	615
21700	188	306	418	510	27000	240	398	506	617
21800	189	307	420	512	27100	241	400	508	619
21900	191	309	422	515	27200	242	402	509	621
22000	192	310	424	517	27300	243	403	511	623
22100	194	311	425	519	27400	244	405	512	625
22200	195	312	427	521	27500	245	407	514	627
22300	196	313	429	523	27600	246	409	516	629
22400	197	315	430	525	27700	246	411	518	630
22500	198	316	432	527	27800	247	413	521	632

Income ($)	Monthly Award ($) No. of Children				Income ($)	Monthly Award ($) No. of Children			
	1	2	3	4		1	2	3	4
27900	248	415	523	634	33200	291	483	637	738
28000	249	416	525	636	33300	291	484	639	741
28100	250	418	527	638	33400	292	486	640	743
28200	251	420	529	640	33500	293	487	642	746
28300	252	422	532	642	33600	294	488	643	748
28400	253	424	534	644	33700	295	489	645	751
28500	254	426	536	646	33800	296	491	647	753
28600	254	428	538	647	33900	296	492	648	756
28700	255	429	540	649	34000	297	493	650	758
28800	256	430	543	651	34100	298	494	651	761
28900	257	432	545	653	34200	299	496	653	763
29000	258	433	547	655	34300	300	497	655	766
29100	259	434	549	657	34400	301	498	656	768
29200	260	436	551	659	34500	301	499	658	771
29300	261	437	554	661	34600	302	501	659	773
29400	261	439	556	662	34700	303	502	661	776
29500	262	440	558	664	34800	304	503	663	778
29600	263	441	560	666	34900	304	504	664	781
29700	264	442	562	668	35000	305	506	666	783
29800	265	443	564	669	35100	306	507	667	786
29900	265	444	566	670	35200	307	508	669	788
30000	266	446	568	672	35300	308	509	671	791
30100	267	447	570	673	35400	308	511	672	793
30200	267	448	572	674	35500	309	512	674	796
30300	268	449	575	675	35600	310	513	675	798
30400	269	450	577	677	35700	311	514	677	801
30500	269	451	579	678	35800	311	516	679	803
30600	270	452	581	679	35900	312	517	680	806
30700	271	453	583	681	36000	313	518	682	809
30800	272	454	585	682	36100	314	520	683	811
30900	272	455	587	684	36200	315	521	685	814
31000	273	456	589	685	36300	315	522	687	816
31100	274	458	591	688	36400	316	523	688	819
31200	275	459	594	690	36500	317	525	690	821
31300	275	460	596	692	36600	318	526	692	824
31400	276	461	598	695	36700	319	527	693	827
31500	277	462	600	697	36800	319	529	695	829
31600	278	463	602	699	36900	320	530	697	832
31700	278	465	604	702	37000	321	531	698	834
31800	279	466	606	704	37100	322	533	700	837
31900	280	467	608	706	37200	323	534	702	839
32000	281	468	611	709	37300	324	535	703	841
32100	281	469	613	711	37400	324	537	705	843
32200	282	470	615	714	37500	325	538	707	845
32300	283	472	617	716	37600	326	539	708	847
32400	284	473	620	718	37700	327	540	710	849
32500	285	474	622	721	37800	328	542	712	851
32600	286	476	624	723	37900	328	543	713	853
32700	286	477	627	726	38000	329	544	715	855
32800	287	478	629	728	38100	330	546	717	857
32900	288	479	631	731	38200	331	547	718	859
33000	289	481	633	733	38300	332	548	720	861
33100	290	482	635	736	38400	332	549	722	862

Income ($)	Monthly Award ($)				Income ($)	Monthly Award ($)			
	No. of Children					No. of Children			
	1	2	3	4		1	2	3	4
38500	333	551	723	864	43800	377	619	813	971
38600	334	552	725	866	43900	378	621	814	973
38700	335	553	727	868	44000	379	622	816	975
38800	336	554	728	870	44100	380	623	818	977
38900	337	556	730	872	44200	381	624	819	979
39000	337	557	732	874	44300	382	626	821	981
39100	338	558	733	876	44400	382	627	823	983
39200	339	559	735	878	44500	383	628	824	985
39300	340	561	737	880	44600	384	630	826	987
39400	341	562	738	882	44700	385	631	828	989
39500	341	563	740	884	44800	386	632	829	991
39600	342	564	742	886	44900	387	634	831	993
39700	343	566	743	888	45000	387	635	833	995
39800	344	567	745	890	45100	388	636	834	997
39900	345	568	747	892	45200	389	637	836	999
40000	345	570	748	894	45300	390	639	838	1001
40100	346	571	750	896	45400	391	640	840	1003
40200	347	572	752	898	45500	392	641	841	1005
40300	348	573	753	900	45600	392	643	843	1007
40400	349	575	755	902	45700	393	644	845	1009
40500	350	576	757	904	45800	394	645	846	1011
40600	350	577	759	906	45900	395	647	848	1013
40700	351	579	760	908	46000	396	648	850	1015
40800	352	580	762	910	46100	397	649	851	1017
40900	353	581	764	912	46200	398	651	853	1019
41000	354	583	765	914	46300	398	652	855	1021
41100	355	584	767	916	46400	399	653	856	1023
41200	356	585	769	918	46500	400	654	858	1025
41300	356	587	771	920	46600	401	656	860	1027
41400	357	588	772	922	46700	402	657	861	1029
41500	358	589	774	924	46800	403	658	863	1031
41600	359	590	776	926	46900	403	660	865	1032
41700	360	592	777	928	47000	404	661	866	1034
41800	361	593	779	930	47100	405	662	868	1036
41900	361	594	781	932	47200	406	664	870	1038
42000	362	596	782	934	47300	407	665	871	1040
42100	363	597	784	936	47400	408	666	873	1042
42200	364	598	786	938	47500	408	668	875	1044
42300	365	600	787	940	47600	409	669	876	1046
42400	366	601	789	942	47700	410	670	878	1048
42500	366	602	791	944	47800	411	671	880	1050
42600	367	604	792	946	47900	412	673	882	1052
42700	368	605	794	948	48000	413	674	883	1054
42800	369	606	796	950	48100	413	675	885	1056
42900	370	607	798	952	48200	414	677	887	1058
43000	371	609	799	954	48300	415	678	888	1060
43100	371	610	801	956	48400	416	679	890	1062
43200	372	611	803	958	48500	417	681	892	1064
43300	373	613	804	960	48600	418	682	893	1066
43400	374	614	806	962	48700	419	683	895	1068
43500	375	615	808	964	48800	419	685	897	1070
43600	376	617	809	966	48900	420	686	898	1072
43700	377	618	811	969	49000	421	687	900	1074

Income ($)	Monthly Award ($) No. of Children				Income ($)	Monthly Award ($) No. of Children			
	1	2	3	4		1	2	3	4
49100	422	688	902	1076	54400	464	755	988	1178
49200	423	690	903	1078	54500	465	756	989	1180
49300	424	691	905	1080	54600	465	757	991	1182
49400	424	692	907	1082	54700	466	758	992	1184
49500	425	694	908	1084	54800	467	760	994	1186
49600	426	695	910	1086	54900	467	761	996	1188
49700	427	696	912	1088	55000	468	762	997	1189
49800	428	698	913	1090	55100	469	763	999	1191
49900	429	699	915	1092	55200	470	764	1000	1193
50000	429	700	917	1094	55300	470	766	1002	1195
50100	430	702	918	1096	55400	471	767	1003	1197
50200	431	703	920	1098	55500	472	768	1005	1199
50300	432	704	922	1100	55600	472	769	1006	1200
50400	433	705	924	1102	55700	473	770	1008	1202
50500	434	707	925	1104	55800	474	771	1009	1204
50600	434	708	927	1106	55900	475	773	1011	1206
50700	435	709	929	1108	56000	475	774	1013	1208
50800	436	711	930	1110	56100	476	775	1014	1210
50900	437	712	932	1112	56200	477	776	1016	1212
51000	438	713	934	1114	56300	478	778	1017	1214
51100	439	715	935	1116	56400	479	779	1019	1215
51200	440	716	937	1118	56500	479	780	1021	1217
51300	440	717	939	1120	56600	480	781	1022	1219
51400	441	719	940	1122	56700	481	783	1024	1221
51500	442	720	942	1124	56800	482	784	1025	1223
51600	443	721	944	1126	56900	483	785	1027	1225
51700	444	722	945	1128	57000	483	786	1029	1227
51800	445	724	947	1130	57100	484	788	1030	1229
51900	445	725	949	1132	57200	485	789	1032	1231
52000	446	726	950	1134	57300	486	790	1033	1233
52100	447	728	952	1136	57400	487	791	1035	1234
52200	448	729	954	1138	57500	488	793	1037	1236
52300	449	730	955	1140	57600	488	794	1038	1238
52400	450	731	957	1142	57700	489	795	1040	1240
52500	450	733	959	1143	57800	490	796	1042	1242
52600	451	734	960	1145	57900	491	798	1043	1244
52700	452	735	962	1147	58000	492	799	1045	1246
52800	452	736	963	1149	58100	492	800	1046	1248
52900	453	737	965	1151	58200	493	801	1048	1250
53000	454	739	966	1153	58300	494	803	1050	1252
53100	455	740	968	1154	58400	495	804	1051	1253
53200	455	741	969	1156	58500	496	805	1053	1255
53300	456	742	971	1158	58600	496	806	1054	1257
53400	457	743	972	1160	58700	497	808	1056	1259
53500	457	744	974	1162	58800	498	809	1058	1261
53600	458	746	976	1164	58900	499	810	1059	1263
53700	459	747	977	1165	59000	500	811	1061	1265
53800	460	748	979	1167	59100	500	813	1062	1267
53900	460	749	980	1169	59200	501	814	1064	1269
54000	461	750	982	1171	59300	502	815	1065	1270
54100	462	751	983	1173	59400	503	816	1067	1272
54200	462	753	985	1175	59500	503	817	1068	1274
54300	463	754	986	1177	59600	504	818	1070	1276

Income ($)	Monthly Award ($)				Income ($)	Monthly Award ($)			
	No. of Children					No. of Children			
	1	2	3	4		1	2	3	4
59700	505	820	1071	1277	65000	543	879	1148	1368
59800	506	821	1073	1279	65100	543	880	1150	1370
59900	506	822	1074	1281	65200	544	881	1151	1371
60000	507	823	1076	1283	65300	544	882	1152	1373
60100	508	824	1077	1284	65400	545	883	1153	1374
60200	509	825	1079	1286	65500	545	884	1154	1376
60300	509	826	1080	1288	65600	546	885	1156	1377
60400	510	828	1082	1290	65700	546	886	1157	1379
60500	511	829	1083	1291	65800	547	886	1158	1380
60600	511	830	1085	1293	65900	547	887	1159	1382
60700	512	831	1086	1295	66000	548	888	1160	1383
60800	513	832	1088	1297	66100	548	889	1162	1385
60900	514	833	1089	1298	66200	549	890	1163	1386
61000	514	834	1091	1300	66300	549	891	1164	1388
61100	515	836	1092	1302	66400	550	892	1165	1389
61200	516	837	1093	1303	66500	550	893	1166	1390
61300	517	838	1095	1305	66600	551	894	1168	1392
61400	517	839	1096	1307	66700	552	895	1169	1393
61500	518	840	1098	1309	66800	552	895	1170	1395
61600	519	841	1099	1310	66900	553	896	1171	1396
61700	520	843	1101	1312	67000	553	897	1173	1398
61800	520	844	1102	1314	67100	554	898	1174	1399
61900	521	845	1104	1316	67200	554	899	1175	1401
62000	522	846	1105	1317	67300	555	900	1176	1402
62100	523	847	1107	1319	67400	555	901	1178	1404
62200	523	848	1108	1321	67500	556	902	1179	1405
62300	524	849	1110	1323	67600	556	903	1180	1407
62400	525	851	1111	1324	67700	557	904	1181	1408
62500	525	852	1113	1326	67800	558	905	1183	1410
62600	526	853	1114	1328	67900	558	906	1184	1411
62700	527	854	1116	1330	68000	559	907	1185	1413
62800	528	855	1117	1331	68100	559	908	1186	1414
62900	528	856	1119	1333	68200	560	909	1188	1416
63000	529	857	1120	1335	68300	560	910	1189	1417
63100	530	859	1121	1337	68400	561	911	1190	1419
63200	531	860	1123	1338	68500	562	912	1192	1421
63300	531	861	1124	1340	68600	562	913	1193	1422
63400	532	862	1126	1342	68700	563	914	1194	1424
63500	533	863	1127	1344	68800	564	915	1196	1425
63600	533	864	1129	1345	68900	564	916	1197	1427
63700	534	865	1130	1347	69000	565	917	1198	1428
63800	535	866	1132	1348	69100	566	918	1200	1430
63900	535	867	1133	1350	69200	566	919	1201	1432
64000	536	868	1134	1352	69300	567	920	1202	1433
64100	537	870	1136	1353	69400	568	921	1204	1435
64200	537	871	1137	1355	69500	568	922	1205	1436
64300	538	872	1138	1357	69600	569	923	1206	1438
64400	539	873	1140	1358	69700	570	924	1208	1440
64500	539	874	1141	1360	69800	570	925	1209	1441
64600	540	875	1143	1362	69900	571	926	1210	1443
64700	541	876	1144	1363	70000	572	927	1212	1444
64800	541	877	1145	1365	70100	572	928	1213	1446
64900	542	878	1147	1367	70200	573	929	1214	1447

Income ($)	Monthly Award ($) No. of Children				Income ($)	Monthly Award ($) No. of Children			
	1	2	3	4		1	2	3	4
70300	574	930	1216	1449	75600	609	986	1287	1533
70400	574	931	1217	1451	75700	610	987	1288	1535
70500	575	932	1218	1452	75800	611	988	1289	1536
70600	576	934	1220	1454	75900	611	989	1291	1538
70700	576	935	1221	1455	76000	612	990	1292	1539
70800	577	936	1222	1457	76100	613	991	1293	1541
70900	578	937	1224	1459	76200	613	992	1295	1542
71000	578	938	1225	1460	76300	614	993	1296	1544
71100	579	939	1226	1462	76400	615	994	1297	1546
71200	580	940	1228	1463	76500	615	995	1299	1547
71300	581	941	1229	1465	76600	616	996	1300	1549
71400	581	942	1230	1466	76700	617	997	1301	1550
71500	582	943	1232	1468	76800	617	998	1303	1552
71600	583	944	1233	1470	76900	618	999	1304	1554
71700	583	945	1234	1471	77000	619	1000	1305	1555
71800	584	946	1236	1473	77100	619	1001	1307	1557
71900	585	947	1237	1474	77200	620	1002	1308	1558
72000	585	948	1238	1476	77300	621	1003	1309	1560
72100	586	949	1240	1478	77400	621	1004	1311	1561
72200	587	950	1241	1479	77500	622	1005	1312	1563
72300	587	951	1242	1481	77600	623	1006	1313	1565
72400	588	952	1244	1482	77700	623	1007	1315	1566
72500	589	953	1245	1484	77800	624	1009	1316	1568
72600	589	954	1246	1485	77900	625	1010	1317	1569
72700	590	955	1248	1487	78000	625	1011	1319	1571
72800	591	956	1249	1489	78100	626	1012	1320	1573
72900	591	957	1250	1490	78200	627	1013	1321	1574
73000	592	959	1252	1492	78300	627	1014	1323	1576
73100	593	960	1253	1493	78400	628	1015	1324	1577
73200	593	961	1255	1495	78500	629	1016	1325	1579
73300	594	962	1256	1497	78600	629	1017	1327	1580
73400	595	963	1257	1498	78700	630	1018	1328	1582
73500	595	964	1259	1500	78800	631	1019	1330	1584
73600	596	965	1260	1501	78900	631	1020	1331	1585
73700	597	966	1261	1503	79000	632	1021	1332	1587
73800	597	967	1263	1504	79100	633	1022	1334	1588
73900	598	968	1264	1506	79200	633	1023	1335	1590
74000	599	969	1265	1508	79300	634	1024	1336	1592
74100	599	970	1267	1509	79400	635	1025	1338	1593
74200	600	971	1268	1511	79500	635	1026	1339	1595
74300	601	972	1269	1512	79600	636	1027	1340	1596
74400	601	973	1271	1514	79700	637	1028	1342	1598
74500	602	974	1272	1516	79800	637	1029	1343	1599
74600	603	975	1273	1517	79900	638	1030	1344	1601
74700	603	976	1275	1519	80000	639	1031	1346	1603
74800	604	977	1276	1520	80100	639	1032	1347	1604
74900	605	978	1277	1522	80200	640	1034	1348	1606
75000	605	979	1279	1523	80300	641	1035	1350	1607
75100	606	980	1280	1525	80400	641	1036	1351	1609
75200	607	981	1281	1527	80500	642	1037	1352	1611
75300	607	982	1283	1528	80600	643	1038	1354	1612
75400	608	984	1284	1530	80700	643	1039	1355	1614
75500	609	985	1285	1531	80800	644	1040	1356	1615

Income ($)	Monthly Award ($) No. of Children				Income ($)	Monthly Award ($) No. of Children			
	1	2	3	4		1	2	3	4
80900	645	1041	1358	1617	86200	680	1096	1429	1701
81000	645	1042	1359	1618	86300	681	1097	1430	1702
81100	646	1043	1360	1620	86400	682	1098	1431	1704
81200	647	1044	1362	1622	86500	682	1099	1433	1705
81300	647	1045	1363	1623	86600	683	1100	1434	1707
81400	648	1046	1364	1625	86700	684	1101	1435	1709
81500	649	1047	1366	1626	86800	684	1102	1437	1710
81600	649	1048	1367	1628	86900	685	1103	1438	1712
81700	650	1049	1368	1630	87000	686	1104	1439	1713
81800	651	1050	1370	1631	87100	686	1105	1441	1715
81900	651	1051	1371	1633	87200	687	1106	1442	1717
82000	652	1052	1372	1634	87300	688	1107	1443	1718
82100	653	1053	1374	1636	87400	688	1109	1445	1720
82200	654	1054	1375	1637	87500	689	1110	1446	1721
82300	654	1055	1376	1639	87600	690	1111	1447	1723
82400	655	1056	1378	1641	87700	690	1112	1449	1724
82500	656	1057	1379	1642	87800	691	1113	1450	1726
82600	656	1059	1380	1644	87900	692	1114	1451	1728
82700	657	1060	1382	1645	88000	692	1115	1453	1729
82800	658	1061	1383	1647	88100	693	1116	1454	1731
82900	658	1062	1384	1649	88200	694	1117	1455	1732
83000	659	1063	1386	1650	88300	694	1118	1457	1734
83100	660	1064	1387	1652	88400	695	1119	1458	1736
83200	660	1065	1388	1653	88500	696	1120	1459	1737
83300	661	1066	1390	1655	88600	696	1121	1461	1739
83400	662	1067	1391	1656	88700	697	1122	1462	1740
83500	662	1068	1392	1658	88800	698	1123	1463	1742
83600	663	1069	1394	1660	88900	698	1124	1465	1743
83700	664	1070	1395	1661	89000	699	1125	1466	1745
83800	664	1071	1396	1663	89100	700	1126	1467	1747
83900	665	1072	1398	1664	89200	700	1127	1469	1748
84000	666	1073	1399	1666	89300	701	1128	1470	1750
84100	666	1074	1400	1668	89400	702	1129	1471	1751
84200	667	1075	1402	1669	89500	702	1130	1473	1753
84300	668	1076	1403	1671	89600	703	1131	1474	1755
84400	668	1077	1405	1672	89700	704	1132	1476	1756
84500	669	1078	1406	1674	89800	704	1134	1477	1758
84600	670	1079	1407	1675	89900	705	1135	1478	1759
84700	670	1080	1409	1677	90000	706	1136	1480	1761
84800	671	1081	1410	1679	90100	706	1137	1481	1762
84900	672	1082	1411	1680	90200	707	1138	1482	1764
85000	672	1084	1413	1682	90300	708	1139	1484	1766
85100	673	1085	1414	1683	90400	708	1140	1485	1767
85200	674	1086	1415	1685	90500	709	1141	1486	1769
85300	674	1087	1417	1687	90600	710	1142	1488	1770
85400	675	1088	1418	1688	90700	710	1143	1489	1772
85500	676	1089	1419	1690	90800	711	1144	1490	1774
85600	676	1090	1421	1691	90900	712	1145	1492	1775
85700	677	1091	1422	1693	91000	712	1146	1493	1777
85800	678	1092	1423	1694	91100	713	1147	1494	1778
85900	678	1093	1425	1696	91200	714	1148	1496	1780
86000	679	1094	1426	1698	91300	714	1149	1497	1781
86100	680	1095	1427	1699	91400	715	1150	1498	

Income ($)	Monthly Award ($) No. of Children				Income ($)	Monthly Award ($) No. of Children			
	1	2	3	4		1	2	3	4
91500	716	1151	1500	1785	96800	751	1206	1571	1869
91600	716	1152	1501	1786	96900	752	1207	1572	1870
91700	717	1153	1502	1788	97000	753	1209	1573	1872
91800	718	1154	1504	1789	97100	753	1210	1575	1873
91900	718	1155	1505	1791	97200	754	1211	1576	1875
92000	719	1156	1506	1793	97300	755	1212	1577	1876
92100	720	1157	1508	1794	97400	755	1213	1579	1878
92200	720	1159	1509	1796	97500	756	1214	1580	1880
92300	721	1160	1510	1797	97600	757	1215	1581	1881
92400	722	1161	1512	1799	97700	757	1216	1583	1883
92500	722	1162	1513	1800	97800	758	1217	1584	1884
92600	723	1163	1514	1802	97900	759	1218	1585	1886
92700	724	1164	1516	1804	98000	759	1219	1587	1888
92800	724	1165	1517	1805	98100	760	1220	1588	1889
92900	725	1166	1518	1807	98200	761	1221	1589	1891
93000	726	1167	1520	1808	98300	761	1222	1591	1892
93100	726	1168	1521	1810	98400	762	1223	1592	1894
93200	727	1169	1522	1812	98500	763	1224	1593	1895
93300	728	1170	1524	1813	98600	763	1225	1595	1897
93400	729	1171	1525	1815	98700	764	1226	1596	1899
93500	729	1172	1526	1816	98800	765	1227	1597	1900
93600	730	1173	1528	1818	98900	765	1228	1599	1902
93700	731	1174	1529	1819	99000	766	1229	1600	1903
93800	731	1175	1530	1821	99100	767	1230	1601	1905
93900	732	1176	1532	1823	99200	767	1231	1603	1907
94000	733	1177	1533	1824	99300	768	1233	1604	1908
94100	733	1178	1534	1826	99400	769	1234	1605	1910
94200	734	1179	1536	1827	99500	769	1235	1607	1911
94300	735	1180	1537	1829	99600	770	1236	1608	1913
94400	735	1181	1538	1831	99700	771	1237	1609	1914
94500	736	1182	1540	1832	99800	771	1238	1611	1916
94600	737	1184	1541	1834	99900	772	1239	1612	1918
94700	737	1185	1542	1835	100000	773	1240	1613	1919
94800	738	1186	1544	1837	100100	773	1241	1615	1921
94900	739	1187	1545	1838	100200	774	1242	1616	1922
95000	739	1188	1546	1840	100300	775	1243	1617	1924
95100	740	1189	1548	1842	100400	775	1244	1619	1926
95200	741	1190	1549	1843	100500	776	1245	1620	1927
95300	741	1191	1551	1845	100600	777	1246	1621	1929
95400	742	1192	1552	1846	100700	777	1247	1623	1930
95500	743	1193	1553	1848	100800	778	1248	1624	1932
95600	743	1194	1555	1850	100900	779	1249	1626	1933
95700	744	1195	1556	1851	101000	779	1250	1627	1935
95800	745	1196	1557	1853	101100	780	1251	1628	1937
95900	745	1197	1559	1854	101200	781	1252	1630	1938
96000	746	1198	1560	1856	101300	781	1253	1631	1940
96100	747	1199	1561	1857	101400	782	1254	1632	1941
96200	747	1200	1563	1859	101500	783	1255	1634	1943
96300	748	1201	1564	1861	101600	783	1256	1635	1945
96400	749	1202	1565	1862	101700	784	1258	1636	1946
96500	749	1203	1567	1864	101800	785	1259	1638	1948
96600	750	1204	1568	1865	101900	785	1260	1639	1949
96700	751	1205	1569	1867	102000	786	1261	1640	1951

Income ($)	Monthly Award ($)				Income ($)	Monthly Award ($)			
	No. of Children					No. of Children			
	1	2	3	4		1	2	3	4
102100	787	1262	1642	1952	107400	822	1317	1713	2036
102200	787	1263	1643	1954	107500	823	1318	1714	2038
102300	788	1264	1644	1956	107600	824	1319	1715	2039
102400	789	1265	1646	1957	107700	824	1320	1717	2041
102500	789	1266	1647	1959	107800	825	1321	1718	2043
102600	790	1267	1648	1960	107900	826	1322	1719	2044
102700	791	1268	1650	1962	108000	826	1323	1721	2046
102800	791	1269	1651	1964	108100	827	1324	1722	2047
102900	792	1270	1652	1965	108200	828	1325	1723	2049
103000	793	1271	1654	1967	108300	828	1326	1725	2051
103100	793	1272	1655	1968	108400	829	1327	1726	2052
103200	794	1273	1656	1970	108500	830	1328	1727	2054
103300	795	1274	1658	1971	108600	830	1329	1729	2055
103400	795	1275	1659	1973	108700	831	1330	1730	2057
103500	796	1276	1660	1975	108800	832	1331	1731	2058
103600	797	1277	1662	1976	108900	832	1333	1733	2060
103700	797	1278	1663	1978	109000	833	1334	1734	2062
103800	798	1279	1664	1979	109100	834	1335	1735	2063
103900	799	1280	1666	1981	109200	834	1336	1737	2065
104000	799	1281	1667	1983	109300	835	1337	1738	2066
104100	800	1283	1668	1984	109400	836	1338	1739	2068
104200	801	1284	1670	1986	109500	836	1339	1741	2070
104300	802	1285	1671	1987	109600	837	1340	1742	2071
104400	802	1286	1672	1989	109700	838	1341	1743	2073
104500	803	1287	1674	1990	109800	838	1342	1745	2074
104600	804	1288	1675	1992	109900	839	1343	1746	2076
104700	804	1289	1676	1994	110000	840	1344	1747	2077
104800	805	1290	1678	1995	110100	840	1345	1749	2079
104900	806	1291	1679	1997	110200	841	1346	1750	2081
105000	806	1292	1680	1998	110300	842	1347	1751	2082
105100	807	1293	1682	2000	110400	842	1348	1753	2084
105200	808	1294	1683	2002	110500	843	1349	1754	2085
105300	808	1295	1684	2003	110600	844	1350	1755	2087
105400	809	1296	1686	2005	110700	844	1351	1757	2089
105500	810	1297	1687	2006	110800	845	1352	1758	2090
105600	810	1298	1688	2008	110900	846	1353	1759	2092
105700	811	1299	1690	2009	111000	846	1354	1761	2093
105800	812	1300	1691	2011	111100	847	1355	1762	2095
105900	812	1301	1692	2013	111200	848	1356	1763	2096
106000	813	1302	1694	2014	111300	848	1358	1765	2098
106100	814	1303	1695	2016	111400	849	1359	1766	2100
106200	814	1304	1697	2017	111500	850	1360	1767	2101
106300	815	1305	1698	2019	111600	850	1361	1769	2103
106400	816	1306	1699	2020	111700	851	1362	1770	2104
106500	816	1308	1701	2022	111800	852	1363	1772	2106
106600	817	1309	1702	2024	111900	852	1364	1773	2108
106700	818	1310	1703	2025	112000	853	1365	1774	2109
106800	818	1311	1705	2027	112100	854	1366	1776	2111
106900	819	1312	1706	2028	112200	854	1367	1777	2112
107000	820	1313	1707	2030	112300	855	1368	1778	2114
107100	820	1314	1709	2032	112400	856	1369	1780	2115
107200	821	1315	1710	2033	112500	856	1370	1781	2117
107300	822	1316	1711	2035	112600	857	1371	1782	2119

Income ($)	Monthly Award ($) No. of Children				Income ($)	Monthly Award ($) No. of Children			
	1	2	3	4		1	2	3	4
112700	858	1372	1784	2120	118000	893	1427	1855	2204
112800	858	1373	1785	2122	118100	894	1428	1856	2206
112900	859	1374	1786	2123	118200	895	1429	1857	2207
113000	860	1375	1788	2125	118300	895	1430	1859	2209
113100	860	1376	1789	2127	118400	896	1431	1860	2210
113200	861	1377	1790	2128	118500	897	1433	1861	2212
113300	862	1378	1792	2130	118600	897	1434	1863	2214
113400	862	1379	1793	2131	118700	898	1435	1864	2215
113500	863	1380	1794	2133	118800	899	1436	1865	2217
113600	864	1381	1796	2134	118900	899	1437	1867	2218
113700	864	1383	1797	2136	119000	900	1438	1868	2220
113800	865	1384	1798	2138	119100	901	1439	1869	2222
113900	866	1385	1800	2139	119200	901	1440	1871	2223
114000	866	1386	1801	2141	119300	902	1441	1872	2225
114100	867	1387	1802	2142	119400	903	1442	1873	2226
114200	868	1388	1804	2144	119500	903	1443	1875	2228
114300	868	1389	1805	2146	119600	904	1444	1876	2229
114400	869	1390	1806	2147	119700	905	1445	1877	2231
114500	870	1391	1808	2149	119800	905	1446	1879	2233
114600	870	1392	1809	2150	119900	906	1447	1880	2234
114700	871	1393	1810	2152	120000	907	1448	1881	2236
114800	872	1394	1812	2153	120100	907	1449	1883	2237
114900	872	1395	1813	2155	120200	908	1450	1884	2239
115000	873	1396	1814	2157	120300	909	1451	1885	2241
115100	874	1397	1816	2158	120400	909	1452	1887	2242
115200	874	1398	1817	2160	120500	910	1453	1888	2244
115300	875	1399	1818	2161	120600	911	1454	1889	2245
115400	876	1400	1820	2163	120700	911	1455	1891	2247
115500	877	1401	1821	2165	120800	912	1456	1892	2248
115600	877	1402	1822	2166	120900	913	1458	1893	2250
115700	878	1403	1824	2168	121000	913	1459	1895	2252
115800	879	1404	1825	2169	121100	914	1460	1896	2253
115900	879	1405	1826	2171	121200	915	1461	1897	2255
116000	880	1406	1828	2172	121300	915	1462	1899	2256
116100	881	1408	1829	2174	121400	916	1463	1900	2258
116200	881	1409	1830	2176	121500	917	1464	1901	2260
116300	882	1410	1832	2177	121600	917	1465	1903	2261
116400	883	1411	1833	2179	121700	918	1466	1904	2263
116500	883	1412	1834	2180	121800	919	1467	1905	2264
116600	884	1413	1836	2182	121900	919	1468	1907	2266
116700	885	1414	1837	2184	122000	920	1469	1908	2267
116800	885	1415	1838	2185	122100	921	1470	1909	2269
116900	886	1416	1840	2187	122200	921	1471	1911	2271
117000	887	1417	1841	2188	122300	922	1472	1912	2272
117100	887	1418	1842	2190	122400	923	1473	1913	2274
117200	888	1419	1844	2191	122500	923	1474	1915	2275
117300	889	1420	1845	2193	122600	924	1475	1916	2277
117400	889	1421	1847	2195	122700	925	1476	1917	2279
117500	890	1422	1848	2196	122800	925	1477	1919	2280
117600	891	1423	1849	2198	122900	926	1478	1920	2282
117700	891	1424	1851	2199	123000	927	1479	1922	2283
117800	892	1425	1852	2201	123100	927	1480	1923	2285
117900	893	1426	1853	2203	123200	928	1481	1924	2286

Income ($)	Monthly Award ($)				Income ($)	Monthly Award ($)			
	No. of Children					No. of Children			
	1	2	3	4		1	2	3	4
123300	929	1483	1926	2288	128600	964	1538	1997	2372
123400	929	1484	1927	2290	128700	965	1539	1998	2373
123500	930	1485	1928	2291	128800	966	1540	1999	2375
123600	931	1486	1930	2293	128900	966	1541	2001	2377
123700	931	1487	1931	2294	129000	967	1542	2002	2378
123800	932	1488	1932	2296	129100	968	1543	2003	2380
123900	933	1489	1934	2298	129200	968	1544	2005	2381
124000	933	1490	1935	2299	129300	969	1545	2006	2383
124100	934	1491	1936	2301	129400	970	1546	2007	2385
124200	935	1492	1938	2302	129500	970	1547	2009	2386
124300	935	1493	1939	2304	129600	971	1548	2010	2388
124400	936	1494	1940	2305	129700	972	1549	2011	2389
124500	937	1495	1942	2307	129800	972	1550	2013	2391
124600	937	1496	1943	2309	129900	973	1551	2014	2392
124700	938	1497	1944	2310	130000	974	1552	2015	2394
124800	939	1498	1946	2312	130100	974	1553	2017	2396
124900	939	1499	1947	2313	130200	975	1554	2018	2397
125000	940	1500	1948	2315	130300	976	1555	2019	2399
125100	941	1501	1950	2316	130400	976	1556	2021	2400
125200	941	1502	1951	2318	130500	977	1558	2022	2402
125300	942	1503	1952	2320	130600	978	1559	2023	2404
125400	943	1504	1954	2321	130700	978	1560	2025	2405
125500	943	1505	1955	2323	130800	979	1561	2026	2407
125600	944	1506	1956	2324	130900	980	1562	2027	2408
125700	945	1508	1958	2326	131000	980	1563	2029	2410
125800	945	1509	1959	2328	131100	981	1564	2030	2411
125900	946	1510	1960	2329	131200	982	1565	2031	2413
126000	947	1511	1962	2331	131300	982	1566	2033	2415
126100	947	1512	1963	2332	131400	983	1567	2034	2416
126200	948	1513	1964	2334	131500	984	1568	2035	2418
126300	949	1514	1966	2335	131600	984	1569	2037	2419
126400	950	1515	1967	2337	131700	985	1570	2038	2421
126500	950	1516	1968	2339	131800	986	1571	2039	2423
126600	951	1517	1970	2340	131900	986	1572	2041	2424
126700	952	1518	1971	2342	132000	987	1573	2042	2426
126800	952	1519	1972	2343	132100	988	1574	2043	2427
126900	953	1520	1974	2345	132200	988	1575	2045	2429
127000	954	1521	1975	2347	132300	989	1576	2046	2430
127100	954	1522	1976	2348	132400	990	1577	2047	2432
127200	955	1523	1978	2350	132500	990	1578	2049	2434
127300	956	1524	1979	2351	132600	991	1579	2050	2435
127400	956	1525	1980	2353	132700	992	1580	2051	2437
127500	957	1526	1982	2354	132800	992	1581	2053	2438
127600	958	1527	1983	2356	132900	993	1583	2054	2440
127700	958	1528	1984	2358	133000	994	1584	2055	2442
127800	959	1529	1986	2359	133100	994	1585	2057	2443
127900	960	1530	1987	2361	133200	995	1586	2058	2445
128000	960	1531	1988	2362	133300	996	1587	2059	2446
128100	961	1533	1990	2364	133400	996	1588	2061	2448
128200	962	1534	1991	2366	133500	997	1589	2062	2449
128300	962	1535	1993	2367	133600	998	1590	2063	2451
128400	963	1536	1994	2369	133700	998	1591	2065	2453
128500	964	1537	1995	2370	133800	999	1592	2066	2454

Income ($)	Monthly Award ($)				Income ($)	Monthly Award ($)			
	No. of Children					No. of Children			
	1	2	3	4		1	2	3	4
133900	1000	1593	2068	2456	138000	1027	1636	2122	2521
134000	1000	1594	2069	2457	138100	1028	1637	2124	2522
134100	1001	1595	2070	2459	138200	1029	1638	2125	2524
134200	1002	1596	2072	2461	138300	1029	1639	2126	2525
134300	1002	1597	2073	2462	138400	1030	1640	2128	2527
134400	1003	1598	2074	2464	138500	1031	1641	2129	2529
134500	1004	1599	2076	2465	138600	1031	1642	2130	2530
134600	1004	1600	2077	2467	138700	1032	1643	2132	2532
134700	1005	1601	2078	2468	138800	1033	1644	2133	2533
134800	1006	1602	2080	2470	138900	1033	1645	2134	2535
134900	1006	1603	2081	2472	139000	1034	1646	2136	2537
135000	1007	1604	2082	2473	139100	1035	1647	2137	2538
135100	1008	1605	2084	2475	139200	1035	1648	2138	2540
135200	1008	1606	2085	2476	139300	1036	1649	2140	2541
135300	1009	1608	2086	2478	139400	1037	1650	2141	2543
135400	1010	1609	2088	2480	139500	1037	1651	2143	2544
135500	1010	1610	2089	2481	139600	1038	1652	2144	2546
135600	1011	1611	2090	2483	139700	1039	1653	2145	2548
135700	1012	1612	2092	2484	139800	1039	1654	2147	2549
135800	1012	1613	2093	2486	139900	1040	1655	2148	2551
135900	1013	1614	2094	2487	140000	1041	1656	2149	2552
136000	1014	1615	2096	2489	140100	1041	1658	2151	2554
136100	1014	1616	2097	2491	140200	1042	1659	2152	2556
136200	1015	1617	2098	2492	140300	1043	1660	2153	2557
136300	1016	1618	2100	2494	140400	1043	1661	2155	2559
136400	1016	1619	2101	2495	140500	1044	1662	2156	2560
136500	1017	1620	2102	2497	140600	1045	1663	2157	2562
136600	1018	1621	2104	2499	140700	1045	1664	2159	2563
136700	1018	1622	2105	2500	140800	1046	1665	2160	2565
136800	1019	1623	2106	2502	140900	1047	1666	2161	2567
136900	1020	1624	2108	2503	141000	1047	1667	2163	2568
137000	1020	1625	2109	2505	141100	1048	1668	2164	2570
137100	1021	1626	2110	2506	141200	1049	1669	2165	2571
137200	1022	1627	2112	2508	141300	1049	1670	2167	2573
137300	1023	1628	2113	2510	141400	1050	1671	2168	2575
137400	1023	1629	2114	2511	141500	1051	1672	2169	2576
137500	1024	1630	2116	2513	141600	1051	1673	2171	2578
137600	1025	1631	2117	2514	141700	1052	1674	2172	2579
137700	1025	1633	2118	2516	141800	1053	1675	2173	2581
137800	1026	1634	2120	2518	141900	1053	1676	2175	2582
137900	1027	1635	2121	2519	142000	1054	1677	2176	2584

Income ($)	Monthly Award ($) No. of Children				Income ($)	Monthly Award ($) No. of Children			
	1	2	3	4		1	2	3	4
142100	1055	1678	2177	2586	146200	1082	1721	2232	2650
142200	1055	1679	2179	2587	146300	1083	1722	2234	2652
142300	1056	1680	2180	2589	146400	1083	1723	2235	2654
142400	1057	1681	2181	2590	146500	1084	1724	2236	2655
142500	1057	1683	2183	2592	146600	1085	1725	2238	2657
142600	1058	1684	2184	2594	146700	1085	1726	2239	2658
142700	1059	1685	2185	2595	146800	1086	1727	2240	2660
142800	1059	1686	2187	2597	146900	1087	1728	2242	2662
142900	1060	1687	2188	2598	147000	1087	1729	2243	2663
143000	1061	1688	2189	2600	147100	1088	1730	2244	2665
143100	1061	1689	2191	2601	147200	1089	1731	2246	2666
143200	1062	1690	2192	2603	147300	1089	1733	2247	2668
143300	1063	1691	2193	2605	147400	1090	1734	2248	2669
143400	1063	1692	2195	2606	147500	1091	1735	2250	2671
143500	1064	1693	2196	2608	147600	1091	1736	2251	2673
143600	1065	1694	2197	2609	147700	1092	1737	2252	2674
143700	1065	1695	2199	2611	147800	1093	1738	2254	2676
143800	1066	1696	2200	2612	147900	1093	1739	2255	2677
143900	1067	1697	2201	2614	148000	1094	1740	2256	2679
144000	1067	1698	2203	2616	148100	1095	1741	2258	2681
144100	1068	1699	2204	2617	148200	1095	1742	2259	2682
144200	1069	1700	2205	2619	148300	1096	1743	2260	2684
144300	1069	1701	2207	2620	148400	1097	1744	2262	2685
144400	1070	1702	2208	2622	148500	1098	1745	2263	2687
144500	1071	1703	2209	2624	148600	1098	1746	2264	2688
144600	1071	1704	2211	2625	148700	1099	1747	2266	2690
144700	1072	1705	2212	2627	148800	1100	1748	2267	2692
144800	1073	1706	2214	2628	148900	1100	1749	2268	2693
144900	1073	1708	2215	2630	149000	1101	1750	2270	2695
145000	1074	1709	2216	2631	149100	1102	1751	2271	2696
145100	1075	1710	2218	2633	149200	1102	1752	2272	2698
145200	1075	1711	2219	2635	149300	1103	1753	2274	2700
145300	1076	1712	2220	2636	149400	1104	1754	2275	2701
145400	1077	1713	2222	2638	149500	1104	1755	2276	2703
145500	1077	1714	2223	2639	149600	1105	1756	2278	2704
145600	1078	1715	2224	2641	149700	1106	1758	2279	2706
145700	1079	1716	2226	2643	149800	1106	1759	2280	2707
145800	1079	1717	2227	2644	149900	1107	1760	2282	2709
145900	1080	1718	2228	2646	150000	1108	1761	2283	2711
146000	1081	1719	2230	2647					
146100	1081	1720	2231	2649					

Income	Monthly Award ($)	
	one child	**two children**
For income over $150,000	1108 plus 0.67% of income over $150,000	1761 plus 1.04% of income over $150,000
	three children	**four children**
	2283 plus 1.34% of income over $150,000	2711 plus 1.58% of income over $150,000

Appendix D: Net Worth Statement

Assets (what you own)	Amount
Chequing/savings account(s)	$ _____
Investments (mutual funds, GICs, etc.)	$ _____
Value of home	$ _____
Value of other property	$ _____
Value of automobile(s)	$ _____
Cash value of life insurance	$ _____
RRSP(s)	$ _____
Business interests	$ _____
Other	$ _____
Total Assets	$ _____

Liabilities (what you owe)	Amount
Mortgage(s)	$ _____
Loan(s)	$ _____
Personal line(s) of credit	$ _____
Credit card(s)	$ _____
Unpaid bills	$ _____
Taxes owed	$ _____
Other debts	$ _____
Total Liabilities	$ _____

Net Worth (assets – liabilities)	$ _____

Appendix E: Spending Plan

For annual amounts, such as insurance and car license, divide the yearly amount by 12. Please indicate date due when an expense is paid quarterly, semi-annually, or annually.

Housing	Budget	Actual	Difference
Housing	**Budget**	**Actual**	**Difference**
Rent or mortgage payment (and condo fees)	$ _____	$ _____	$ _____
Property taxes (municipal, school, water, etc.)	$ _____	$ _____	$ _____
Electricity	$ _____	$ _____	$ _____
Heat	$ _____	$ _____	$ _____
Maintenance and repairs (service contracts)	$ _____	$ _____	$ _____
Cable	$ _____	$ _____	$ _____
Telephone	$ _____	$ _____	$ _____
Insurance (fire, liability, contents)	$ _____	$ _____	$ _____
Transportation			
Car payment (loan, lease)	$ _____	$ _____	$ _____
Gas and oil	$ _____	$ _____	$ _____
Repairs and maintenance	$ _____	$ _____	$ _____
Insurance and license	$ _____	$ _____	$ _____
Parking	$ _____	$ _____	$ _____
Public transportation	$ _____	$ _____	$ _____
Taxi	$ _____	$ _____	$ _____
Medical and Dental			
Insurance (life and health premiums)	$ _____	$ _____	$ _____
Expenses (prescription, optometrist, etc.)	$ _____	$ _____	$ _____
Over-the-counter	$ _____	$ _____	$ _____
Living Expenses			
Groceries (food, personal care, cleaning)	$ _____	$ _____	$ _____
Daily purchases (milk, bread, etc.)	$ _____	$ _____	$ _____
Clothes (self)	$ _____	$ _____	$ _____
Clothes (children)	$ _____	$ _____	$ _____
Child care	$ _____	$ _____	$ _____

Books, subscriptions	$ _____	$ _____	$ _____
Entertainment (meals, movies, dues, sports)	$ _____	$ _____	$ _____
Spending money	$ _____	$ _____	$ _____
Miscellaneous (haircuts, pet care, etc.)	$ _____	$ _____	$ _____
Interests and Hobbies	$ _____	$ _____	$ _____
Family (gifts, financial aid, etc.)	$ _____	$ _____	$ _____
Vacation and Travel	$ _____	$ _____	$ _____
Charitable Donations	$ _____	$ _____	$ _____

Credit Payments (excluding mortgages)

Loan(s)	$ _____	$ _____	$ _____
Personal Line of Credit	$ _____	$ _____	$ _____
Credit card(s)	$ _____	$ _____	$ _____
Store financing	$ _____	$ _____	$ _____
Other	$ _____	$ _____	$ _____

Other Expenses

Legal and accounting	$ _____	$ _____	$ _____
Club/union dues	$ _____	$ _____	$ _____
Alimony/child support	$ _____	$ _____	$ _____
Other	$ _____	$ _____	$ _____

Contingency Fund

Emergencies	$ _____	$ _____	$ _____
Capital expenditures (appliances, car, etc.)	$ _____	$ _____	$ _____
Savings	$ _____	$ _____	$ _____

Taxes	$ _____	$ _____	$ _____

Total Monthly Expenses	$ _____	$ _____	$ _____

Employment Income
Spousal Support
Child Support
Other Income
Reimbursement (medical plans, etc.)

Total Income
Less Total Expenses

Difference

Index